500
CROSS STITCH
CHARTED DESIGNS

JULIE HASLER

Text by

VALERIE JANITCH

David & Charles

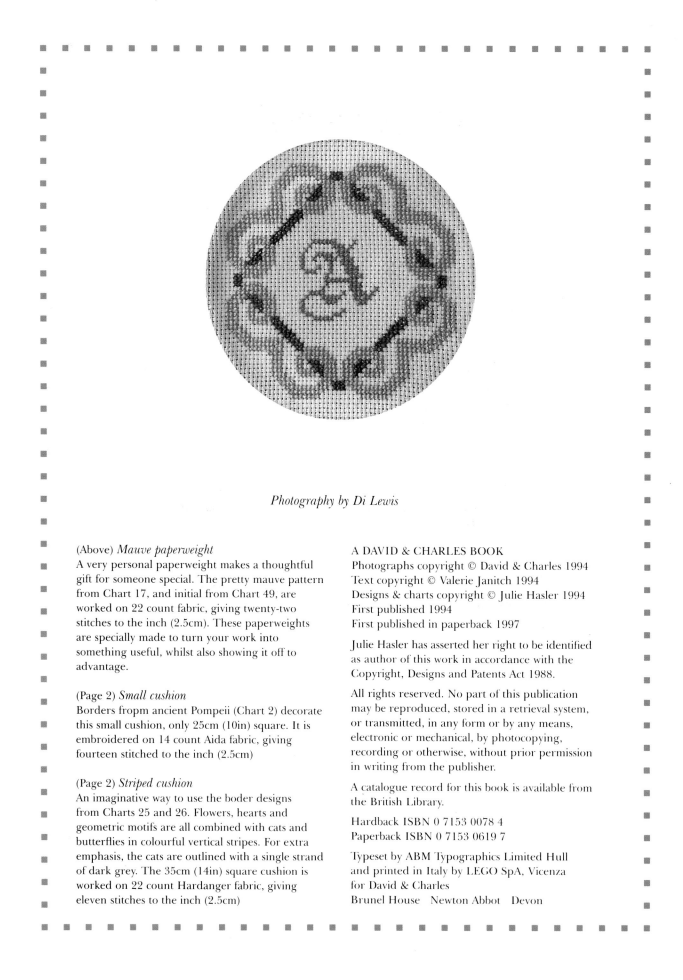

Photography by Di Lewis

(Above) *Mauve paperweight*
A very personal paperweight makes a thoughtful gift for someone special. The pretty mauve pattern from Chart 17, and initial from Chart 49, are worked on 22 count fabric, giving twenty-two stitches to the inch (2.5cm). These paperweights are specially made to turn your work into something useful, whilst also showing it off to advantage.

(Page 2) *Small cushion*
Borders fropm ancient Pompeii (Chart 2) decorate this small cushion, only 25cm (10in) square. It is embroidered on 14 count Aida fabric, giving fourteen stitched to the inch (2.5cm)

(Page 2) *Striped cushion*
An imaginative way to use the boder designs from Charts 25 and 26. Flowers, hearts and geometric motifs are all combined with cats and butterflies in colourful vertical stripes. For extra emphasis, the cats are outlined with a single strand of dark grey. The 35cm (14in) square cushion is worked on 22 count Hardanger fabric, giving eleven stitches to the inch (2.5cm)

A DAVID & CHARLES BOOK
Photographs copyright © David & Charles 1994
Text copyright © Valerie Janitch 1994
Designs & charts copyright © Julie Hasler 1994
First published 1994
First published in paperback 1997

A catalogue record for this book is available from the British Library.

Hardback ISBN 0 7153 0078 4
Paperback ISBN 0 7153 0619 7

Typeset by ABM Typographics Limited Hull
and printed in Italy by LEGO SpA, Vicenza
for David & Charles
Brunel House   Newton Abbot   Devon

CONTENTS

INTRODUCTION

T HIS is not just another book of designs for cross stitch. True, you will find over 500 charted designs buzzing with motifs, borders, alphabets and other ideas that will have you itching to thread a needle.

But the book is much more. What makes this collection uniquely different is the fact that it sets out to inspire as well. And, having done so, it guides your inspiration along practical lines, explaining how to interpret the designs as *you* wish to use them – helping you translate them into things that reflect your own personality.

However you approach your cross stitch project, this book gives you the ability and the freedom to plan and create your own individual embroidery with ease and confidence.

(Opposite) *Framed sampler*
Framed sampler designs make attractive pictures. This one, from Chart 42, is worked on 22 count Hardanger fabric, giving eleven stitches to the inch (2.5cm)

(Below) *Blue tit paperweight*
A tiny blue tit perches on a leafy twig – making an enchanting paperweight. Taken from Chart 92, and stitched with a single strand of embroidery cotton on 18 count cream Aida fabric, giving eighteen stitches to the inch (2.5cm)

1
CREATING YOUR OWN DESIGNS

UPPOSE you wish to make a cushion for your favourite armchair. You will probably have a colour scheme in mind, but you're not sure what kind of design would complement the rest of the room. The curtains and covers are plain, so you wonder whether to try something geometric, perhaps *several* geometric designs, all different, or border patterns, with maybe a single tiny geometric motif in the centre?

Or, if you yearn for something with an air of nostalgia, an embroidered frame to display your wedding photograph makes an enchanting project. It has to be flowers, of that you are certain, but what kind? Roses are the obvious choice, of course; but white carnations or clear blue forget-me-nots are more unusual, and equally romantic. And shall it be one large bloom, two or three smaller ones, or a profusion of tiny blossoms? The choice is endless.

You might be considering a birthday present for a small boy's room. A colourful picture, attractively mounted and framed. The young man loves adventure stories: but how to illustrate his interests in your gift? Perhaps a pirate ship, sailing the high seas, even *several* pirate ships... The embroidery could be as much fun as the finished picture!

Anniversaries, birthdays, Christmas and Easter come round again with increasing frequency, it seems. When you want to let your special friends know how special they are, nothing says it better than an embroidered greetings card. Purchased blank cards in a choice of colours, with different shaped 'windows', provide a perfect mount to display your work. All you need is lots of suggestions for appropriate or festive subjects – as well as some decorative alphabets from which to embroider the recipient's initial or name.

Last but not least, one of the oldest and most popular projections of cross stitch is the sampler. No one can fail to be fascinated by those intriguing examples worked by needlewomen, both young and adult, in previous centuries. Such intensely human documents cry out to be repeated as modern family heirlooms for the next century.

For all those who are anxious to find solutions to similar questions, this book is the embroiderer's equivalent to a cross stitch computer! Motifs for every situation and occasion present themselves at whirlwind speed: your only task is to put all the elements of the design together to create an attractive whole. Follow the directions on page 11 to plan your cushion, frame, picture, card, sampler or any other project – and you can be sure before you begin that you will end up with a carefully planned and co-ordinated result.

Pair of pirate ships picture

A wide coloured mount makes this pair of jolly pirate ships from Chart 72 even more intriguing: just the thing to capture a small boy's imagination. And the embroidery is as much fun as the pictures! Worked in bold colours on a 27 count evenweave cotton, giving 13½ stitches to the inch (2.5cm)

8

Valentine card

The Valentine rabbits from Chart 86 are embroidered on 22 count Hardanger fabric, giving twenty-two stitches to the inch (2.5cm). Set in a blank mount to make a keepsake that the one you love will treasure always. These cards, which come in different sizes and colours, with a variety of 'window' shapes, present your work in the most professional way

Bookmark

An amusing, but useful, gift for the booklover. The rabbits, from an Easter bunny border on Chart 84, are worked alternately in dark and mid brown on 16 count Summer Khaki Aida fabric, giving sixteen stitches to the inch (2.5cm).

The purchased bookmark means that making up afterwards is quick and easy – and you have a very professional result too

HOW TO USE THE SELECTIVE DESIGN PLANNER

At the end of this introductory section – and just before the actual charts begin – you'll find the SELECTIVE DESIGN PLANNER. This is the brilliant device that answers all your questions, and solves all your problems.

You may already know exactly what you want to make, you just need to find the right design or designs to decorate it. Alternatively you might be suffering from that 'itchy-fingers' urge to make *something*, but you want ideas.

Whether you belong to the first category or the second, the procedure couldn't be simpler. Just run your eye down the highly comprehensive and detailed list, either to be inspired with exciting ideas, or to find charted designs for the kind of subject that you already had in mind.

All you need to know in order to interpret your chosen designs, or to translate them into the context you require, is explained in the following pages. How to choose your fabric, how to plan out your design on graph paper, and even how – if you have never cross stitched before – to execute this simple form of embroidery so that you produce a professional-looking piece of work that is as near perfection as possible. This is no idle promise: cross stitch is one of the simplest forms of embroidery ever invented.

This book will stimulate your imagination, so take full advantage of its exciting potential to produce work that is truly your own.

PLANNING WHAT YOU WANT TO MAKE

Once you have decided what you are going to make, the most important consideration is the size of the finished article. This will, in part, determine the size or the amount of design that you will be able to incorporate into your project. A cushion might be 40cm (16in) square; a photograph frame 15 x 10cm (6 x 4in); a book-mark 3cm (1¼in) wide. This will indicate the size of design that you will be looking for.

Having decided the size, you must think about your fabric. The different fabrics available are described in the next chapter, to enable you to choose the one that you feel will be the most suitable for your project. But don't actually buy anything yet. Plan out your design first, basing it on the fabric that you have chosen. Not only will this tell you how much fabric you need to purchase, it will also allow you to change your mind if you find that your design would fit better on another fabric.

Cast your eye over the Selective Design Planner index (see page 40) and jot down on a piece of paper the numbers of any charts that suggest a possible design. Then turn the pages to find the charts that you have noted, and consider each design in the context of what you are going to make.

Although it is not essential to read Chapter 4 before you begin to design, you will probably find it helpful to do so. It may influence your thinking on the dimensions, surplus fabric requirements and general presentation.

CALCULATING THE CHARTED DESIGNS

To do this, count the number of squares (each square represents a stitch) in order to estimate the size of the finished embroidery when it is worked over your chosen fabric. This will either confirm or determine the thread count or type of fabric that you need to buy.

Fabrics are described in detail in the next chapter, where you will see that they produce different sized stitches according to the number of threads or blocks there are to the inch. On an evenweave linen, or cotton, the cross stitch is usually embroidered over two threads in each direction. This means that a fabric with 28 threads to the inch in each direction produces fourteen cross stitches to the inch. (One inch equals 2.5cm – but cross stitch fabrics are generally described in 'threads to the inch' or 'stitches to the inch'.) Other fabrics, such as Aida, are woven in 'blocks', and each cross stitch is worked over one block. So if you count the number of stitches in each direction, you will be able to calculate the size the design would be when worked over different fabrics – bearing in mind the number of stitches to the inch that each particular fabric produces.

For instance, a design that is 42 squares deep and 28 squares wide, if worked on an even-weave linen with twenty-eight threads to the inch (fourteen stitches), will result in an embroidered motif that is 3in (just under 7.6cm) deep by 2in (just under 5cm) wide. The same design, worked over a fabric with *less* threads to the inch will be *larger*: but worked over a fabric with *more* threads to the inch, it will be *smaller*.

As already described, Aida fabrics are woven in blocks, which makes them even easier to calculate: because the number of blocks to the inch is the same as the number of stitches to the inch.

It is very important to be able to visualise your proposed design in proportion to your project, because then you will immediately see if it fits well, and whether the thread count that you have chosen is the most appropriate. You may decide the design should be a little smaller – so choose a higher thread count: alternatively, to enlarge the design, reduce the thread count. Or, you could stay with your original thread count, but choose a design with more or less

Christmas table runner

Teddy Bears and Christmas trees from Chart 75 make a double border for this festive table runner. Worked with two strands over two threads of 26 count evenweave fabric, giving thirteen stitches to the inch (2.5cm). Ready-to-work items like this fringed runner let you enjoy the stitching without having to spend time making it up afterwards

Poinsettia card

The oval mount on this card perfectly frames an attractive design combining two traditional Christmas themes – a lighted candle and the striking poinsettia flower. From Chart 78, this one is worked on 18 count Ainring fabric, giving eighteen stitches to the inch (2.5cm)

Stocking card

A larger card shows off a bright red Christmas stocking, sparkling with frosty white snowflakes. The main design is from Chart 78, and the white stars filling in the background are from Chart 77. Worked on 16 count Aida fabric, giving sixteen stitches to the inch

Christmas bell card

A small blank card mount is the perfect setting for the Christmas bell from Chart 78. Worked on 28 count evenweave cotton, giving fourteen stitches to the inch (2.5cm).

Candle Christmas card

A traditional design for Christmas, from Chart 77. The bright yellow candle flame is emphasised by backstitching with a single strand of the orange embroidery thread used at the centre. The gleaming halo which surrounds it is worked with three strands of light gold thread (Fil or clair).
    Worked on 14 count cream Aida, giving fourteen stitches to the inch (2.5cm)

stitches: or build up an existing design by adding a narrow border or another motif. This is the fun of creating your own design – the more you do it, the more you'll enjoy it. The best way to see how all this works in practice is to plan out a specific design as a working example. But first, a word about measurements.

MEASUREMENTS – IMPERIAL VERSUS METRIC

Working in cross stitch is a little more complicated for those who are accustomed to using metric measurements. Embroidery fabrics, as already mentioned, tend to be calculated to the inch, so remember to work in imperial measure. US readers will, of course, have no problem.

However, in other instances where both metric and imperial measurements are stated, you will notice that the conversions are not accurate. Instead, the designs are calculated individually to give you the convenience of working with straightforward amounts.

DESIGNING YOUR PROJECT

Let's imagine that you are designing a frame for a favourite photograph. You have in mind a mount surrounding a rectangular picture. Your photograph measures approximately 9cm (3½in) deep × 6.5cm (2½in) wide. If the mount has to fit an existing frame, measure and cut out a sheet of graph paper the appropriate size. Place your photograph on this sheet to determine where you want it to be. It could be exactly central (Fig 1a), but it would be better balanced if the surround was the same width at the top and sides, making it a little deeper at the bottom (Fig 1b); or you might decide to have extra height at the top (Fig 1c). However, the picture doesn't have to be in the middle: move it around a bit to see whether you prefer it placed slightly off-centre (Figs 1d and 1e). This position is perfect for a romantic floral design – in which case you might think about showing the photograph as an oval, instead of a rectangle (Fig 1f).

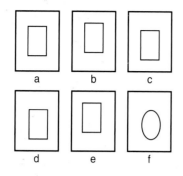

Fig 1   Deciding the options for placing your photograph

Fig 2   Make the window slightly smaller than your photograph

However, if your mount is also acting as the frame itself (as our examples on page 15), you will have more freedom to design if you place your photograph on the graph paper and then work out your embroidery design around it, letting that dictate the actual size and shape of the finished frame. If you decide to do it this way, rule lines around the photograph to give a rough indication of the size and shape you require: then you can adjust it when you have finalised the design.

When you have decided, mark the position of the photograph on the graph paper as indicated by the broken line on Fig 2. Then make the window a little smaller, so that the edges of the photograph will be covered, as indicated by the inner bold line. As you can see, we have chosen the position shown in Fig 1b on a mount measuring approximately 19 × 15cm (7½ × 6in).

Now you are ready to prepare your actual embroidery design sheet: this is the graph paper chart from which you will be working. For something of this nature, a fairly fine, Aida fabric would look very attractive, and also has

the advantage of being very easy to count. So, for the purposes of this explanation, we are working on one with sixteen blocks to the inch – giving sixteen stitches to the inch.

In inches, our mount measures 7½in deep × 6in wide. As each tiny square on your sheet of graph paper represents one stitch, you will have to cut another piece of paper 120 squares deep × 96 squares wide. If, however, you had chosen to work on an Aida fabric with less blocks to the inch – for instance fourteen blocks (14 stitches to the inch) – your graph paper would have to be 105 squares deep × 84 squares wide.

In other words, multiply the actual measurement of your finished work by the number of stitches to the inch, to find the number of squares on your design chart. In the case of our 7½ × 6in mount, we calculated for a fabric with a count of sixteen blocks (16 stitches) to the inch:

$$7\tfrac{1}{2} \times 16 = 120 \text{ squares deep}$$
$$\text{and} \quad 6 \times 16 = 96 \text{ squares wide}$$

Photograph frame

The completed 'Roses' photograph frame described on page 16. It is worked on 16 count Parchment colour Aida fabric, giving sixteen stitches to the inch (2.5cm). Both the main designs are from Chart 28. The very narrow border around the window is taken from the edge of a much wider design on Chart 44. You will often find that you are able to adapt existing charts in this way to suit your own requirements.

It can be seen from the working chart that the border was left until last, and then only a small section was necessary to assess the total effect

Oval photograph frame

The floral arch from Chart 47 makes a perfect setting for a portrait of someone special. The arch is extended by an additional flower and leaf at each side, to accommodate the circular window. This kind of flexibility is yet another advantage of being able to plan your own designs. The frame is 15cm (6in) × 11.5cm (4½in) wide, and is worked on an evenweave cotton with 28 threads (fourteen stitches) to the inch (2.5cm)

But, for an evenweave fabric with twenty-eight threads (14 stitches) to the inch, or a fabric with fourteen blocks (14 stitches) to the inch:

$$7\tfrac{1}{2} \times 14 = 105 \text{ squares deep}$$
$$\text{and} \quad 6 \times 14 = 84 \text{ squares wide}$$

Remember to mark the position of the photograph, working out the measurement in exactly the same way (Fig 3).

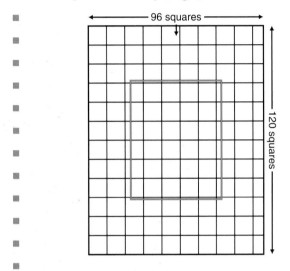

Fig 3 Your design sheet measured out on graph paper, each marked square represents 10 × 10 small squares, ie stitches. The coloured lines mark the window area for the photograph. Note the central point above the window (arrow), where the border embroidery will begin

CHOOSING YOUR EMBROIDERY DESIGNS

Turn to the Selective Design Planner and check out all those charts that suggest a suitable design, as previously described. The full width of the surround in our example is exactly 29 squares at the sides and top, and 38 squares at the base. With this in mind, you are free to make your choice from the enormous range of charted designs on offer.

Copy those you like onto separate pieces of graph paper, then cut them out (allowing an extra square all round) and place them on your design sheet, moving them around to see how they would look. For our example, we have combined two pretty floral borders from Chart 28, with a very narrow edging round the window taken from a wider border on Chart 44. The narrower rosebud border is fitted neatly between the full-blown roses at each top corner, which are balanced by the spray of roses across the base. If you compare the embroidery with the original design on Chart 28, you will notice that a few stitches have been added at each side, extending the leaves to balance the arrangement. Your personal chart allows you to spot small points like this, so that you can improve upon, and perfect the design before you begin to embroider.

Use the strips to decide the positions of the design on your chart. Then, on the chart, mark the centre of the surround at the top (see Fig 3). Mark also the centre of the design on the top strip, and, matching these two points, copy the border from the chart onto the design sheet, working across to the corner, so that it fits: then reverse the design and work across in the other direction to the left hand corner. In this case, the rosebud border is continued down each side only to just below the window. Then the same procedure is followed for the roses across the base: beginning at the centre, the design is taken out to one side and reversed in the other direction (Fig 4).

This is the beauty and joy of the Selective Design Planner. If you know what you want (ie, a wide floral border and a narrow edging) you have only to look for them in the alphabetical index. Or, if you're looking for ideas (ie, something nostalgically romantic) a run down the list of subjects will suggest all the options, and tell you where to find them.

When copying out your design, a set of coloured pencils helps. If you do not have any (or can't borrow them from the children), invent symbols to represent each colour. Remember to list all the symbols on the chart itself, if there is an unused corner – or on a separate sheet, if there is no space. Against each symbol, indicate the colour and, when you have chosen the embroidery threads, identify each with the shade number marked on the paper band.

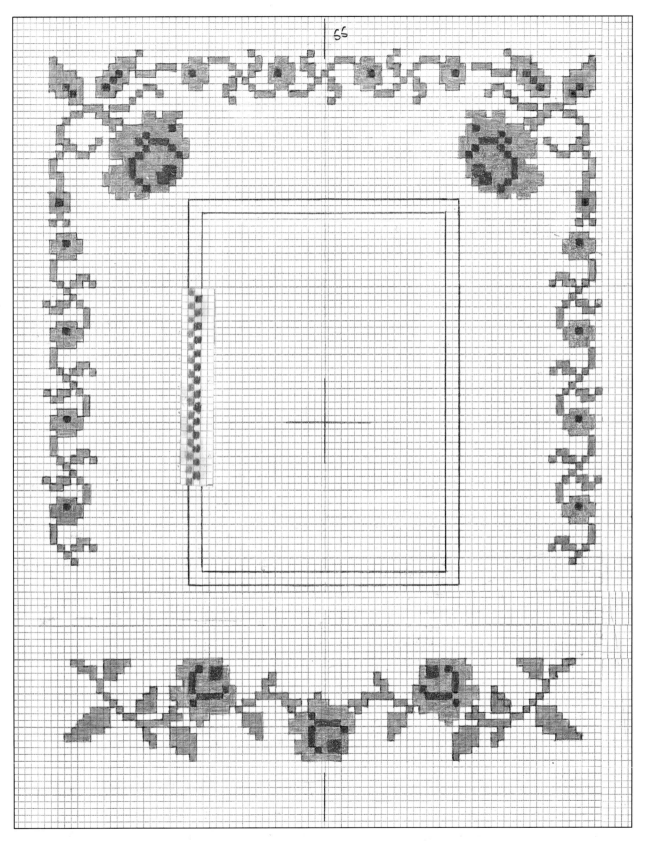

Fig 4   Copy your chosen borders and motifs onto
the graph paper to form a charted design for the
embroidery

2

MATERIALS
AND EQUIPMENT

S ALREADY explained, cross stitch must be worked over an 'even-weave' fabric. This is a fabric that has exactly the same number of threads to the inch in each direction – vertically and horizontally. If this is not the case, your design will be distorted. It may be linen, though this is more expensive, or cotton.

In an evenweave linen fabric, or a cotton, like Linda, the threads are single. In this case, each cross stitch is usually worked over *two* threads in each direction.

Or the threads can be finer, and woven in blocks, like *Aida*, when the cross stitch is worked over a complete block.

Another fabric, *Hardanger*, is a mixture of both the above; it is woven with pairs of finer threads, and the cross stitch usually covers two pairs of threads in each direction.

All the fabrics are available in a good range of colours and a variety of thread counts. Remember that the more crosses to the inch, the smaller your stitches will be. And the fewer crosses to the inch, the larger they will be.

Do be sure to buy enough fabric. You will need to allow 6-8cm (2½-3in) extra all round, depending on the item you are making, and how much you will require for turnings. On the other hand, fabric is expensive so take care to do all your calculations first!

CUTTING AND SEWING

Scissors are a very important item. You'll need a large pair (ideally dressmakers' cutting-out scissors) to cut your fabric. And a pair of small, sharp embroidery scissors is essential. Also, try to have a separate pair with which to cut the paper for your design charts – to prevent blunting the others.

The embroidery is worked with a small blunt tapestry needle (size 24 or 26). Have several needles: keep them in a needle-case or their own special pincushion, and take good care of them.

Although cross stitch may be worked in the

Chick greeting card

The chirpy Easter chick from Chart 84 makes your Eastertide greeting specially personal. Embroidered on 14 count Fine Aida fabric, giving fourteen stitches to the inch (2.5cm)

Easter egg card

A colourful patterned egg set in a cream mount makes a delightful way to say Happy Easter. The design, from Chart 84, is worked on 16 count Aida fabric, giving sixteen stitches to the inch (2.5cm)

Easter card

A small but exquisite card to treasure. The dark blue centre shades out to deep cream against a soft brown ground.

The Easter theme of light coming out of darkness is highlighted by tiny gold cross stitches using two strands of light gold thread (Fil or clair). And this is emphasised by changing the central blue stitches on the original design (Chart 82) to form a circle of gold.

Worked on 16 count Biscuit Aida fabric, giving sixteen stitches to the inch (2.5cm)

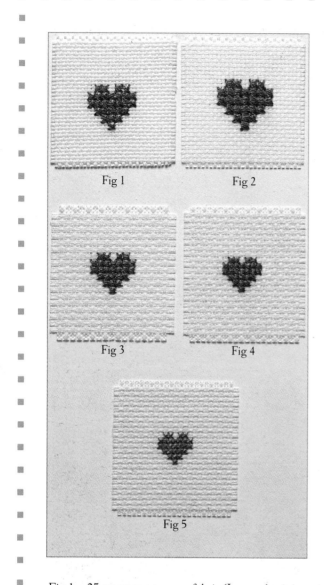

Fig 1   25 count evenweave fabric (Lugana), giving 12½ stitches to the inch (2.5cm): worked with two strands of embroidery thread

Fig 2   22 count Hardanger fabric, giving eleven stitches to the inch (2.5cm): worked with three strands of embroidery thread

Fig 3   14 count Aida fabric, giving fourteen stitches to the inch (2.5cm): worked with two strands of embroidery thread

Fig 4   16 count Aida fabric, giving sixteen stitches to the inch (2.5cm): worked with two strands of embroidery thread

Fig 5   18 count Aida fabric, giving eighteen stitches to the inch (2.5cm): worked with one single strand of embroidery thread

hand, it is easier to achieve a perfectly smooth and even finish if the fabric is absolutely flat, and stretched taut over a hoop. Choose a 10cm (4in), 12.5cm (5in) or 15cm (6in) diameter plastic or wooden hoop, with a screw-type tension adjuster. Larger pieces of embroidery should be worked on a frame. Ask your local needlecraft shop to show you a selection, and advise you.

EMBROIDERY THREADS – STRANDED COTTONS (FLOSS)

Although you will find an interesting choice of threads at your needlecraft shop, six-strand embroidery cotton (floss) is easily the most adaptable and popular medium for cross stitch. DMC stranded embroidery cottons (floss) come in a breathtaking range of shaded colours, so that you can create exciting or subtle colour schemes to your heart's content.

The strands are separated, and the number that you use depends on the fabric: the smaller your crosses, the fewer strands you will need. Two or three strands are the most common number: use two strands for twelve or more stitches to the inch (2.5cm), and three strands for eleven or less stitches.

Silver and gold threads are also available. Used sparingly, these can add attractive highlights to a design, and festive sparkle to a greetings card or Christmas decoration.

PLANNING AND DRAWING OUT DESIGNS

The vital requisite here is graph paper. It doesn't matter whether you buy imperial or metric graph paper, as long as each 1in or 2cm is divided into 10 × 10 tiny squares. There is usually a faint sub-division into 5 × 5 tiny squares: these bolder lines are very helpful in following the design, both when you copy it out, and when you are embroidering. When you copy the design, always follow the heavier lines on the original chart in the book, to avoid mistakes.

You will also need a pencil (well-sharpened),

a soft eraser (essential for every good designer), a ruler and, if possible, a set of coloured pencils.

Whilst you are still making up your mind about your design, use tiny bits of Stick'n'fix adhesive to hold the small pieces of graph paper on the background. This allows you to rearrange everything as often as you like.

An all-purpose clear adhesive like UHU, a latex adhesive like Cow Gum, or a dry stick adhesive like UHU Stic, are all suitable when you want to mount the sections onto your design sheet permanently, to save time actually copying the design onto the sheet. Or you can use a special transparent mending tape, like 3M Magic Scotch tape.

Lavender sachets

The floral initial decorating each of these pretty little scented sachets is taken from the distinctive alphabet on Charts 55-7. The set is a perfect example of how you can ring the changes on a design by altering the colour scheme. The same shade of blue is used to embroider the letter B on three of the sachets, but in each case the subtle colouring of the rose is toned to blend with the background fabric. For the fourth sachet, a paler blue is used to emphasise the initial on the darker fabric. Embroidered on 16 count Aida fabric, giving sixteen stitches to the inch (2.5cm)

3

FOLLOWING YOUR CHART

EFORE you begin, prevent the cut edges of the fabric from ravelling by whip-stitching or machine-stitching all round. Alternatively, turn under and tack a small hem.

FINDING THE CENTRE POINTS

It is usually best to begin stitching at the centre of the fabric – or, if this is not appropriate, at the centre of your design. This ensures that it will be correctly positioned. Fold the fabric in half, first one way and then the other, creasing the folds as you do so. Using contrasting cotton, make a straight, even line of tacking

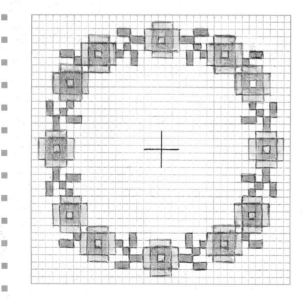

Fig 1   Finding the centre point of the charted design

stitches along each fold, following the woven threads. The point where your two lines cross is the centre.

Then it is necessary to find the centre of your design. To do this, count the squares (stitches) on your chart vertically and horizontally, and divide each figure in half, marking the crossing point as before (Fig 1). Alternatively, measure the chart both ways with a ruler and divide each measurement by 2.

If it is not practical to begin at the centre, count the number of squares/stitches from the centre of your chart to the point where you want to begin: then count an equivalent number of double threads or blocks in the same direction on your fabric.

THREADING YOUR NEEDLE

Cut off a length of cotton – about 45-50cm (18-20in) is a comfortable length to work with. One at a time, gently draw out the number of strands that you require (usually two or three,

Small mosaic trinket box
The mosaic design is taken from Chart 12, and embroidered on 14 count Fine Aida fabric, giving fourteen stitches to the inch (2.5cm), to top a small trinket box

Geometric trinket box
A geometric design from Chart 17 is worked on 22 count Hardanger fabric, giving twenty-two stitches to the inch (2.5cm), for the lid of a charming round trinket box

as explained in Chapter 2), then put the individual strands together again: always do this to ensure a full, neat stitch. Thread the needle, but *don't* make a knot: never use knots to fasten your threads, as they will create bumps at the back that will spoil the smooth surface of your finished work.

Place the remaining strands in a thread holder, which can either be purchased or made from two strips of card between which you have taped small curtain rings (Fig 2). Mark the shade number above each ring.

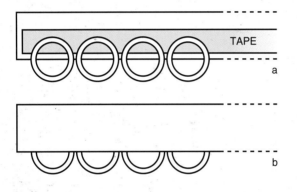

Fig 2 Fix curtain rings between strips of card with double-sided tape, to make a simple home-made thread tidy which saves hours of tangled frustration!

IF YOU ARE USING AN EMBROIDERY HOOP

To place the fabric in the embroidery hoop, rest the area to be embroidered over the inner ring and carefully push the outer ring down over it. Allow approximately 2½in (12cm) larger all round than the size of the outer ring. Pull the fabric gently and evenly, making sure that it is drum taut in the hoop and that the mesh is straight, tightening the screw adjuster as you do so.

When working, you will find it best to have the screw in the 'ten o'clock' position, as this will prevent your thread becoming tangled in the screw with each stitch. If you are left-handed, have the screw in the 'one o'clock' position. As you work, re-tighten the fabric every so often, to keep it taut.

BEGINNING TO CROSS STITCH

All the designs are worked with full cross stitches, although occasionally a half cross is used (forming a triangle, instead of a square). Sometimes a design is outlined in backstitch, which gives it added emphasis, and this facility can also be used most effectively to pick out detail.

As explained in Chapter 2, usually the cross is worked over two threads in each direction of an evenweave linen or cotton like Linda; over a complete block of an Aida fabric; or over two pairs of threads of a Hardanger fabric. If your design incorporates half crosses, you will find it easier to stitch on a fabric where you work over pairs of threads, rather than solid blocks.

Oval jewellery

The small flower from Chart 34 is worked with a single strand over 22 count fabric, giving twenty-two stitches to the inch (2.5cm), and set in an oval silver jewellery mount

Basket of flowers pendant

A basket of flowers from Chart 30 makes an enchanting pendant or brooch when set in a round silver jewellery mount. Worked with a single strand on 18 count Ainring fabric, giving eighteen stitches to the inch (2.5cm)

Art Nouveau trinket box

The elegant Art Noveau flower design from Chart 35 is worked over one block of 22 count Hardanger fabric, using a single strand to give twenty-two stitches to the inch (2.5cm). Matched to a toning base, it makes a beautiful dressing table trinket box

Trinket box

A miniature wreath of golden roses (Chart 28) surrounds an initial in antique script (Chart 51), on the lid of a charming wooden trinket box in toning primrose yellow. The embroidery shown is worked on 16 count cream Aida fabric, giving sixteen stitches to the inch (2.5cm)

Hearts and flowers trinket box

Hearts and flowers (Chart 28) surround an initial from Chart 47. Worked with two strands over 14 count fabric, giving fourteen stitches to the inch (2.5cm)

To begin the first stitch, bring the needle up from the wrong side, through a hole in the fabric at the left hand corner of the stitch (Fig 3); leave a short length underneath and weave it neatly through the backs of the first few stitches, once you have made them (Fig 4).

Next, bring the needle diagonally up across the pairs of threads or block that you want to cover, and take it down through the hole at the right hand corner (Fig 3). This is the first half of your stitch.

The needle is now at the back of the fabric. Take the thread straight down and bring your needle up through the bottom right hand hole (Fig 5): then take the thread diagonally across and up to the remaining corner at the top left, pushing your needle down through it (Fig 5). Your cross stitch is now completed.

This is an individual or isolated stitch. But if you have a horizontal row of stitches in the same colour, work the first half of the stitches all across the line (Fig 6): then return and complete the crosses (Fig 7). Work vertical rows of stitches in the same way (Fig 8).

Finish off your thread on the wrong side, by running your needle under the backs of four or more stitches (Fig 9).

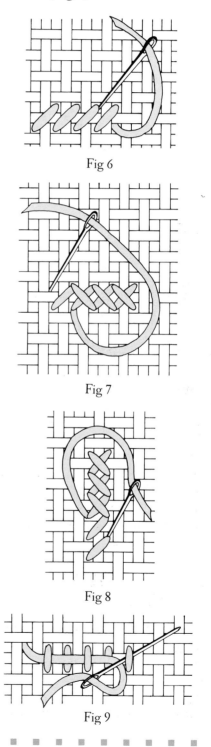

Fig 6

Fig 7

Fig 8

Fig 9

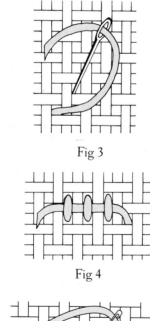

Fig 3

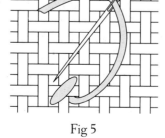

Fig 4

Fig 5

Note: To simplify the working diagrams as much as possible, each vertical and horizontal thread on Figs 3-9 represents a *pair* of threads on an evenweave linen or cotton, a *block* of threads on an Aida fabric, or *two pairs* of threads on a Hardanger fabric.

Sampler greetings cards
Sampler designs from Chart 41 are worked on 22 count Hardanger fabric, giving eleven stitches to the inch (2.5cm), and set in special blank mounts for these decorative greetings cards

OUTLINING AND DETAILING IN BACKSTITCH

Some of the designs are outlined with backstitch to give them greater emphasis. Backstitch is also used to pick out fine details and features.

Always work the backstitch after all the cross stitch embroidery is finished, using one strand less than that used for the cross stitch. For example, if three strands of cotton have been used to work the cross stitch embroidery, use two strands for the backstitching. If two strands were used, use one strand. However, if only one strand of cotton is used to work the cross stitch, one strand is also used for the backstitching.

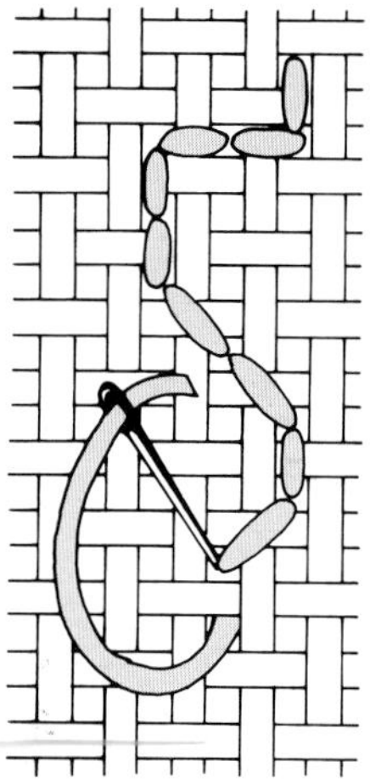

Fig 10

Backstitch is worked from hole to hole, following the same blocks as the cross stitches, and can be stitched in vertical, horizontal or diagonal lines, as Fig 10. Take care not to pull the stitches too tight, or the contrast of colour will be lost. Finish off as for cross stitch.

TURNING CORNERS ON BORDERS

Sometimes it will be obvious how and where to divert the course of a straight border design at a right angle, in order to make a corner. But if you have difficulty deciding how to turn, use a small handbag mirror, positioning it diagonally across the design. Then copy down what you see in the reflection.

USEFUL TIPS FOR A PROFESSIONAL FINISH

When you are stitching, it is important to keep your tension absolutely even: if it is not, it will pull the fabric out of shape. If you are worried about your tension, you can ensure that this doesn't happen by using a hoop (or frame), as described on page 24: then work each stitch by pushing your needle straight up through the fabric, and then straight down again, keeping the fabric smooth and taut. There should be no slack, but don't pull the thread too tight: draw it through so that it lies snug and flat.

If your thread becomes twisted while you are working, drop the needle and let it hang down freely. It will untwist itself. Don't continue working with twisted thread, as it will appear thinner, and won't cover your fabric satisfactorily.

Never leave your needle in the design area of your work when not in use. Not only might it distort the fabric, but no matter how good the needle, it could rust, and leave a permanent mark.

Don't carry threads across the back of an open expanse of fabric. If you are working separate areas of the same colour, finish off and begin again. Loose threads, especially dark colours, will be visible from the right side of your work when the project is finished.

Baby's bib

A pair of plump Teddy Bears from Chart 66 play with their building blocks on this enchanting baby's bib. But they are so simple, a child could make it: what a wonderful gift to work for a small brother or sister! Worked over 14 count waste canvas (fourteen stitches to the inch/2.5cm), which is tacked to the bib before beginning the embroidery. When the cross stitch is finished, the canvas threads are withdrawn

Ladybird babygrow

A flight of bright red ladybirds from Chart 66 alight on a plain babygrow to make it into something really special! Worked over 14 count waste canvas, which is first tacked to the garment, then pulled out, thread-by-thread, once the embroidery is completed

Pirate jeans

Jeans for a seaside holiday sport the pirate flag and seahorse from Chart 71, the starfish from Chart 70 and fish from Chart 69. Worked over 14 count waste canvas, which is tacked to the garment before the embroidery, then drawn out, one thread at a time, when the stitching is finished

Lifeguard T-shirt

The lifebelt from Chart 70 is stitched over 14 count waste canvas to give this T-shirt a suitably nautical air for an aspiring lifeguard. When the embroidery is finished, the canvas threads are pulled away and discarded

4

COMPLETING THE FINISHED PROJECT

WHEN you have completely finished your cross stitch embroidery, it will need to be pressed. Place the fabric right side down on a smooth, softly padded surface or thick towel, then cover the back with a thin, damp cloth before pressing carefully and gently. Leave until it is cool and dry.

TECHNIQUES FOR MAKING UP

There is such a wide range of applications for cross stitch that the methods employed for making up your finished work will be dictated by the item itself. But here are a few general guidelines to ensure a professional finish for some of the most popular projects to which cross stitch is specially suited.

CUSHIONS AND PILLOWS

Although you can make your own inner pads from plain cotton-type fabric and a good quality washable filling material, it is usually more convenient to buy them ready-made, in the size and shape that you require.

As already discussed, you will have had the size and shape in mind when you first planned your cushion or pillow, although when deciding those proportions, it is wise to bear in mind the standard sizes available. Most household department stores and soft furnishing suppliers carry a good range.

Make up your cushion or pillow to the same dimensions as the pad, allowing about 1.5cm (a

good half-inch) extra for the seams. This seam allowance applies if you whip- or machine-stitched the raw edges of your cross stitch fabric before you began the embroidery. However, if you turned under and tacked a small hem instead, take out the tacking threads and either trim the edges to the above seam allowance, and then whip- or machine-stitch them; or if you prefer to leave the edges raw, make the seam allowance a little wider.

Cut your backing fabric the same size as the front of the cushion, then join the two pieces, right sides together, all round, leaving the greater part of one side open at the centre, as Fig 1 – or a similar amount on a round cushion (Fig 2).

For a square or rectangular cushion, mitre

Large blue cushion

Dark blue and turquoise: a tasteful colour scheme for a 40cm (16in) square cushion that combines three borders. Beginning with a broad one round the outer edge (from Chart 32), two more narrow in width as they near the middle (charts 25 and 26): in the centre the eye focuses on a single motif from Chart 18. Worked with three strands of embroidery cotton on 22 count Hardanger fabric, giving eleven stitches to the inch (2.5cm)

Floral cushion

A 35cm (14in) square cushion also worked on 22 count Hardanger fabric, giving eleven stitches to the inch (2.5cm). But in complete contrast, this one takes an old-fashioned floral pattern from Chart 29 for the formal central design, surrounding it prettily with a narrow border from Chart 31

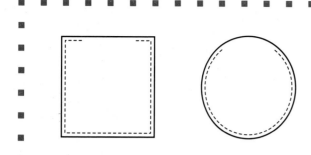

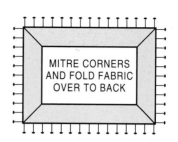

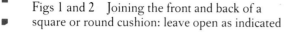

Figs 1 and 2   Joining the front and back of a
square or round cushion: leave open as indicated

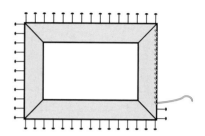

Fig 3   Embroidery stretched over mounting board
and pinned to the edge

Fig 4   Oversewing the fabric to the edge of the
board

the corners (see page 37), then turn to the right
side and press. Insert your cushion pad and
slip-stitch the seam.

For a round cushion, trim and clip the raw
edges of the seam – but not too close to the
stitching. Then turn the seam allowance at
each side of the opening to the wrong side and
tack. Turn the cover to the right side and press.
Insert your cushion pad and slip-stitch the
seam.

A narrow piping cord sewn around the edge
gives cushions a neat and professional
appearance.

SAMPLERS AND PICTURES

These can be framed or not, as you wish, but
choose the frame carefully, if you are having
one, so that it complements your project. A
frame that is too heavy or dark can overwhelm
what it surrounds, whereas a carefully chosen
frame can enhance and emphasise your design.

There is a self-adhesive board available
which is specially made for mounting embroidery. Or you can use an ordinary acid-free stiff
mounting board or foam board. Cut a piece
exactly the size of the actual design – allowing
at least 6-8cm (2½-3in) excess fabric all round,
as directed in the fabrics section of Chapter 2.

You can either stitch the overlapping fabric
to the edge of the board, or lace the surplus at
the back. In either case, place your embroidery
right side up on the board, positioned so that
the edges of the design exactly match the edges
of the board. To do this, mark all round the
edge of the design with a tacking thread, then
pin it carefully to the edge of the board, matching the centres on all four sides before

travelling outwards to the corners with your
pins (Fig 3). Then mitre the corners (see
page 37).

To hold the work permanently, either a)
oversew neatly all round the edge (Fig 4), or b)
use strong linen thread to lace together with
long stitches the two opposite edges of the
surplus fabric, first the top and bottom (Fig 5),
and then the two sides.

For very small projects, you can c) use

Chris

Spell out a child's name with the pictorial alphabet,
and make a colourful sign to hang on their wall or
door. The giant letters are on Charts 58-64: follow
the colours indicated for the letters – or choose
your own, bearing in mind to contrast the colours
of the motif against the letter. In this case, the
letter 'C' was originally purple, but changing it to
orange has added yet another bright colour to the
complete design, instead of repeating the same
colour twice.

Embroidered on 14 count Aida fabric, giving
fourteen stitches to the inch (2.5cm). There are
five blocks between each letter. Two strands of
embroidery thread were used, except for the cat,
which has three strands to give denser coverage

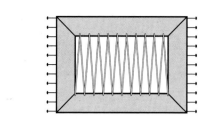

Fig 5   Lacing the top and bottom edges together at the back: then lace the sides together

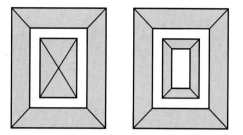

Fig 6   (Left) Make diagonal cuts across the fabric from corner to corner

Fig 7   (Right) Trim away excess at the centre

double-sided tape to secure the excess fabric neatly down over the back. In this case, a transparent mending tape finishes the cut edges neatly, though it isn't necessary.

If you are *not* framing your sampler or picture, follow either methods b) or c) described above. Then cut some cartridge or similar weight paper, or a piece of felt, just a little smaller than the board, and glue it neatly over the back. There are various self-adhesive hanging methods available which can be fixed to the backing.

FRAMES AND MOUNTS

When you are making a frame for a photograph, or an embroidered mount, you will need to cut away a window for the picture. Measure and mark this very carefully on the board, then cut it away with a sharp craft knife and a steel rule. Now stretch the fabric over the board as described above: but before doing so, surround the edges of the picture area with double-sided tape.

If you are following methods a) or c), do the centre after you have completed the whole fabric-fixing operation, (but just before you cover the back with paper or felt). However, if you are using method b), you will have to do the centre and fix your picture after you have pinned the fabric round the edge, but before you lace the back. (If possible, try to avoid method b) for a frame or mount: it complicates the job!)

When the outer edges of the fabric are fixed – methods a) and c) – or pinned – method b) – place the work face down and, for a square or rectangular window, carefully cut a diagonal

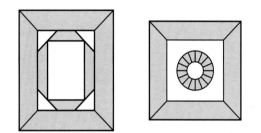

Fig 8   (Left) Turn back and glue to the board

Fig 9   (Right) Cut away a small circle of fabric (or oval following shape of window): then snip the surplus all round

Fig 10   Turn back the tabs and glue to the board

cross from corner to corner of the fabric (Fig 6). Trim away the inner corners of the resulting triangles of fabric (Fig 7), then turn the fabric smoothly and neatly over the cut edges of the card and either tape or glue it to the back (Fig 8).

If the fabric shows a tendency to fray at the corners, use a tiny smear of clear adhesive to secure the woven threads before folding the fabric back.

For a round or oval window, cut away a smaller circle or oval in the centre of the fabric,

then snip the surplus into tiny tabs (Fig 9). One-by-one, turn these tabs smoothly over the edge of the board and glue them to the back (Fig 10).

If you are making a round or oval frame, you will have to employ the same method in reverse to finish the outer edge. Pin the embroidery fabric taut all round the edge of the board, then trim it to shape, leaving a comfortable overlap. Snip out V-shapes all round this surplus, to form tiny tabs (Fig 11). Then fold these tabs smoothly over the edge of the board and glue them to the back (Fig 12).

Double photograph frame

A simple design carried out in a dark colour on a light ground makes a sophisticated surround for a double photograph frame. Embroidered from Chart 25 on 22 count Hardanger fabric, giving eleven stitches to the inch (2.5cm). The frame measures 11 × 16cm (4¼ × 6¼in), and the windows are approximately 7.5 × 5.5cm (3 × 2in)

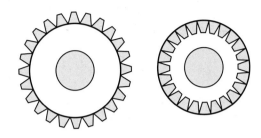

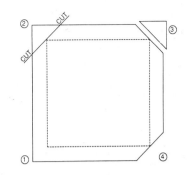

Fig 11   (Left) When the embroidery is pinned, cut surplus fabric to shape round the outer edge and then snip to form V-shaped tabs

Fig 12   (Right) Turn back the tabs and glue to the board

Fig 13   The four stages of mitring a corner

Position the photograph or picture and hold in place with adhesive tape. Cover the back with a slightly larger piece of card, also taped into place. Now finish the back as described for methods a), b) or c), according to the one that you are following.

TO MITRE CORNERS

To avoid bulky corners when folding the raw edges over a stiff backing, cut the corners off diagonally, close to, but not quite touching, the point where the actual corner of the finished item will be (see Fig 13: the broken line represents the completed size of the item). Then fold the surplus to the back and finish as directed.

Square tablecloth

A bold geometric motif from Chart 18 is repeated in the woven squares of Heatherside fabric for this very special tablecloth. Worked over two threads of the 14 count fabric, to give seven stitches to the inch (2.5cm)

Jar lacy pot covers

Lace-edged jar covers for preserves give the tea-table a delightfully old-fashioned air. All you have to do is embroider your design and add a toning ribbon. 18 count Aida in white or cream has eighteen stitches to the inch (2.5cm), and is stitched with a single strand of embroidery thread. The yellow-green pears from Chart 104 have dark green leaves: both pears and leaves are outlined with the dark green. The cherries from Chart 103 have mid green leaves outlined with a slightly darker shade, the cherries themselves are backstitched around with self-colour

TRIMMING THE EDGES

Lace always makes a lovely edging or border for cross stitch, but ribbon can also be used, either in conjunction with lace, or on its own. One specially attractive way to use ribbon is to make a narrow braid by plaiting three lengths of 1.5mm (1/16in) wide satin ribbon. To estimate the amount of ribbon you will need, calculate the length of braid that you require, then add a third of that measurement, and then multiply the result by 3.

If you make an evocative, Victorian-style mount with an oval or circular window, you can add a very pretty touch with a length of tiny pearl beads sewn or glued against the inner edge, just overlapping the photograph. This is also a useful trick if the finished edge of the fabric is not as neat as you would wish.

Hemstitching gives a period feeling, whilst the edges of the fabric can be fringed by working a row of hemstitch before trimming the surplus fabric away to the required length of the fringe and then drawing the threads.

CLEANING AND CARING FOR YOUR CROSS STITCH

Cross stitch embroideries worked on cotton or linen fabrics may be laundered quite safely, if handled with care. For the treatment of work using their stranded embroidery cotton (floss), DMC suggest washing in soapy, warm water. Squeeze without twisting, and hang to dry. Iron the reverse side, using two layers of white linen. Always wash embroidery separately from your other laundry. Avoid dry cleaning.

ACKNOWLEDGEMENTS

I would like to give thanks to the following people for their help with this book: Valerie Janitch for her wonderful writing and editing, Lesley Smith, Patricia Hulance and Dawn Parmley for help and inspiration with design ideas; and Lesley Buckerfield, Jenny Whitlock, Carol Ratcliffe, Barbara Hodgkinson, Odette Harrison, Allison Mortley, Linda Potter, Valerie Janitch and Dawn Parmley for stitching the examples shown in the photographs.

Thanks also to: H. W. Peel & Co. Ltd, Norwester House, Fairway Drive, Greenford, Middlesex, UB6 8PW (for graph paper); Framecraft Miniatures Ltd, 372-376 Summer Lane, Hockley, Birmingham, B19 3QA; and DMC Creative World Ltd, Pullman Road, Wigston, Leicester, LE8 2DY.

(Opposite) *Table linen*

Delft china is suggested by the fresh blue and white colour scheme of the motifs worked on these place mats and tea towels. Embroidered with a single strand over one thread of 26 count evenweave fabric, giving twenty-six stitches to the inch (2.5cm). The coffee pots, vases, rabbit and duck are all from Chart 106

(Below) *Lucky pincushion*

Lucky black cats alternate with white horseshoes on this amusing, but useful, little pincushion. Embroidered from Chart 88 on 16 count dark grey Aida fabric, giving sixteen stitches to the inch

SELECTIVE DESIGN PLANNER

The numbers beside each subject indicate the charts on which such a design (or a suitable design for that occasion) appears.

CHART 1

CHART 2

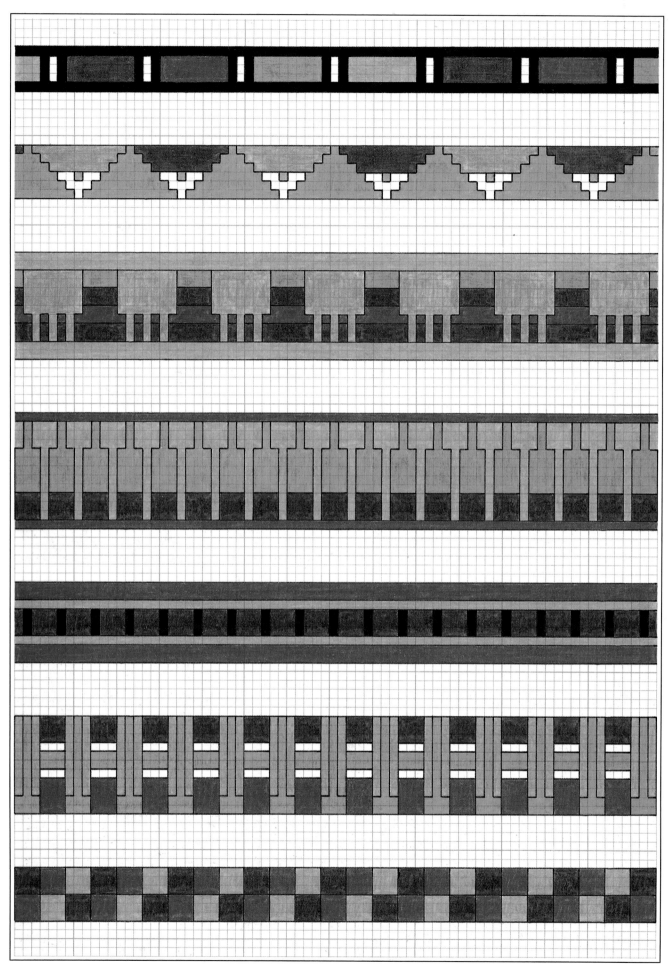

CHART 3

CHART 4

CHART 5

CHART 6

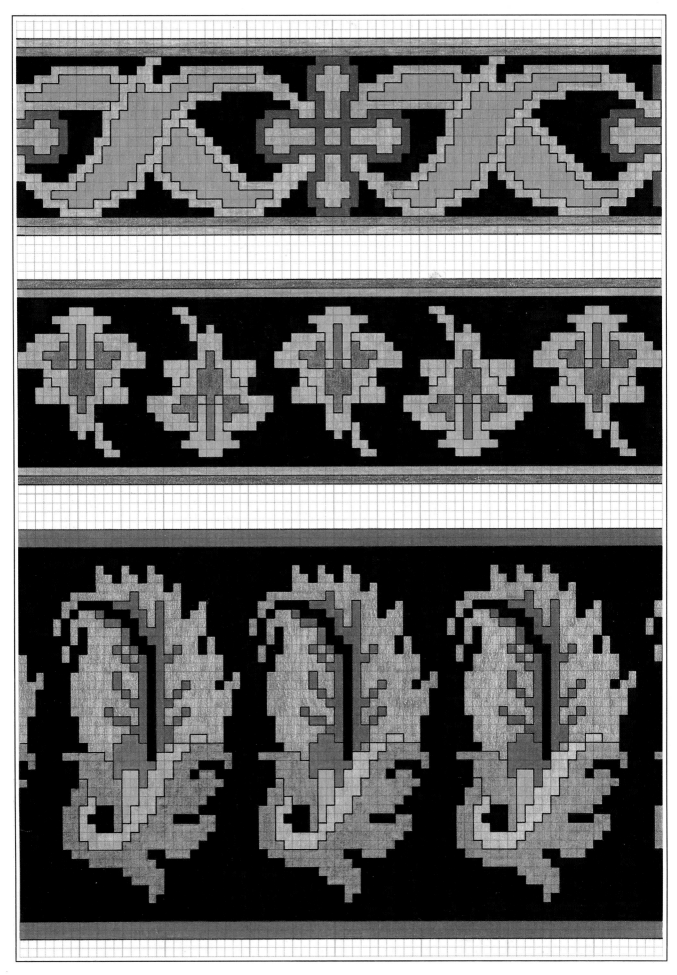

CHART 7

CHART 8

CHART 9

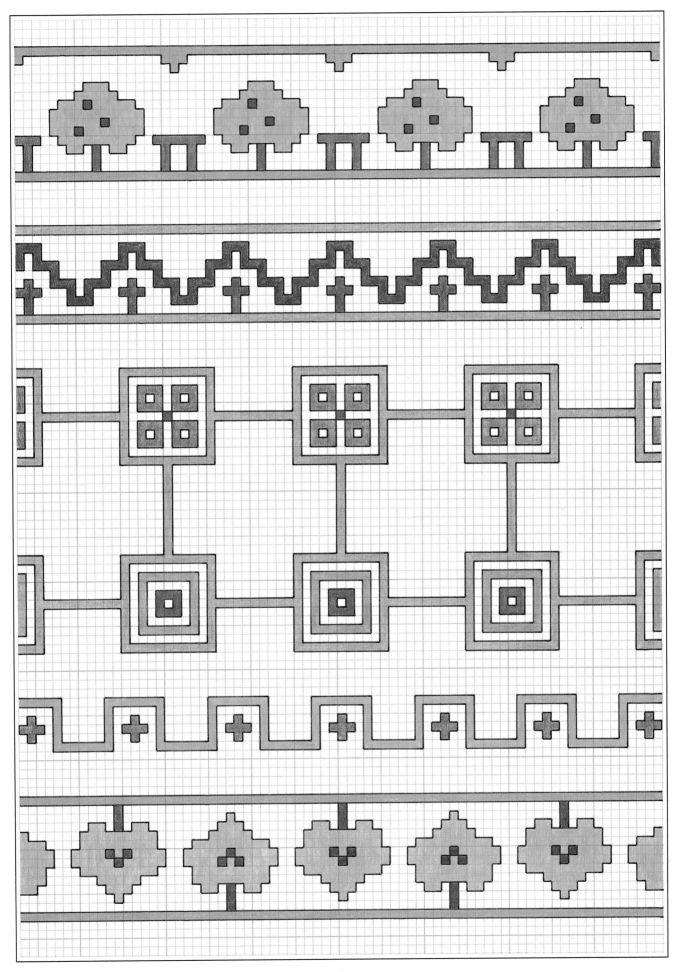

CHART 10

CHART 11

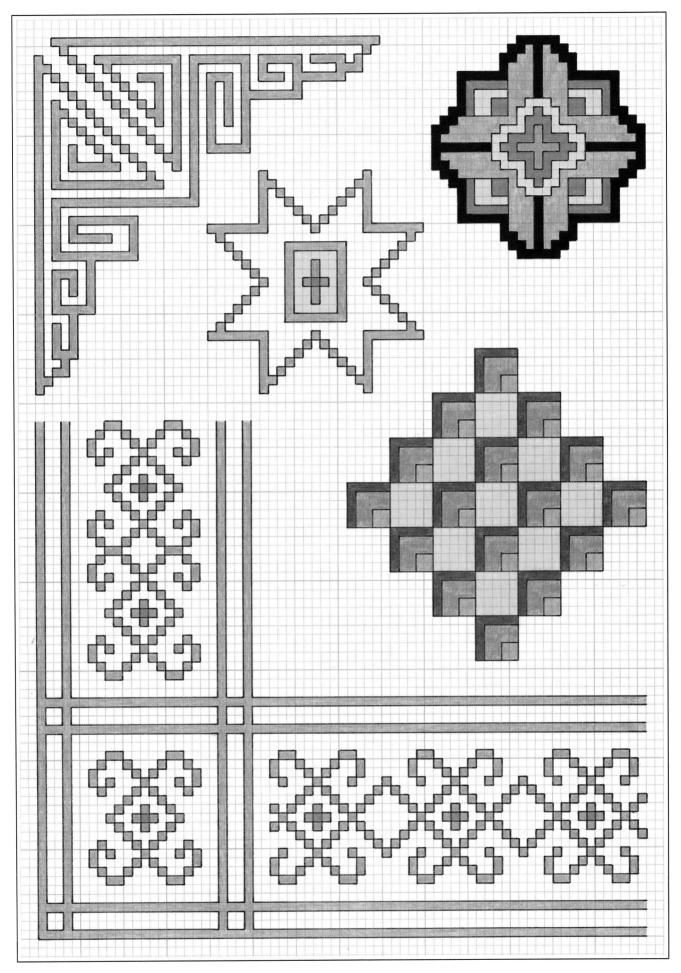

CHART 12

CHART 13

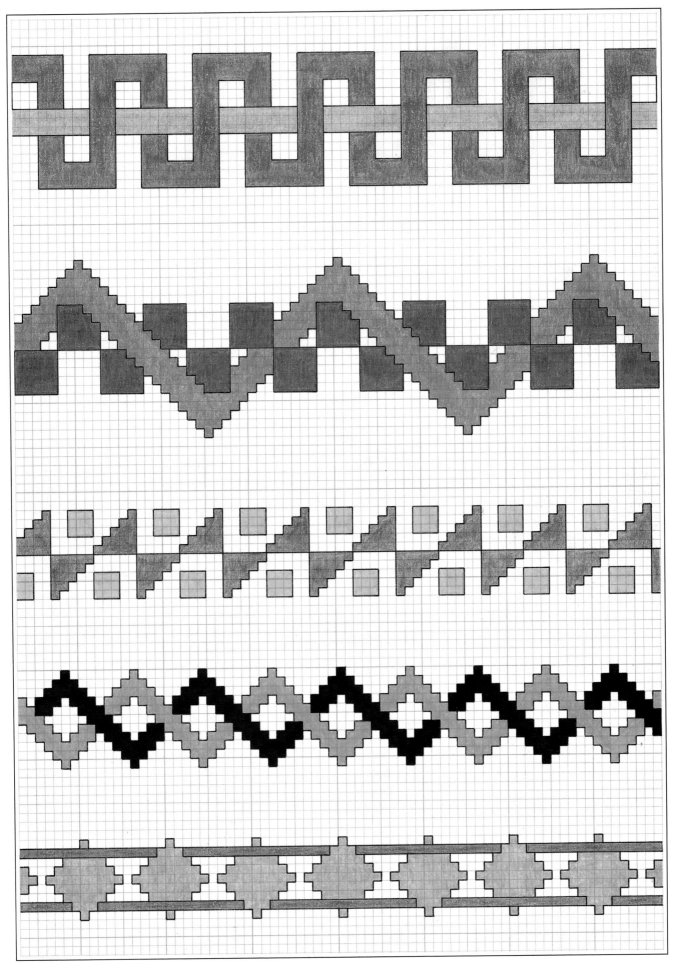

CHART 14

CHART 15

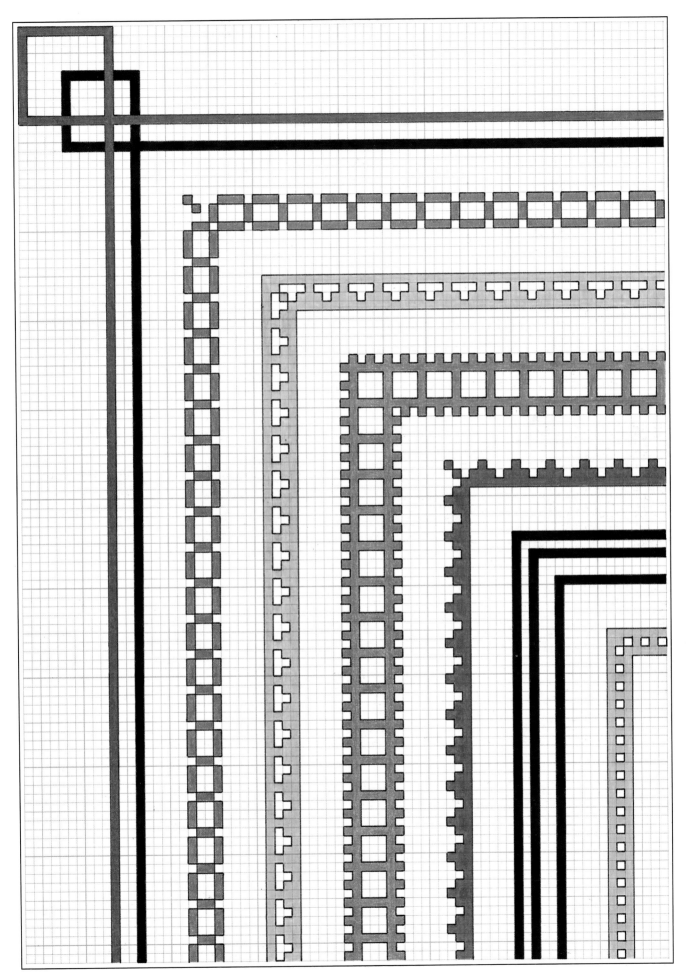

CHART 16

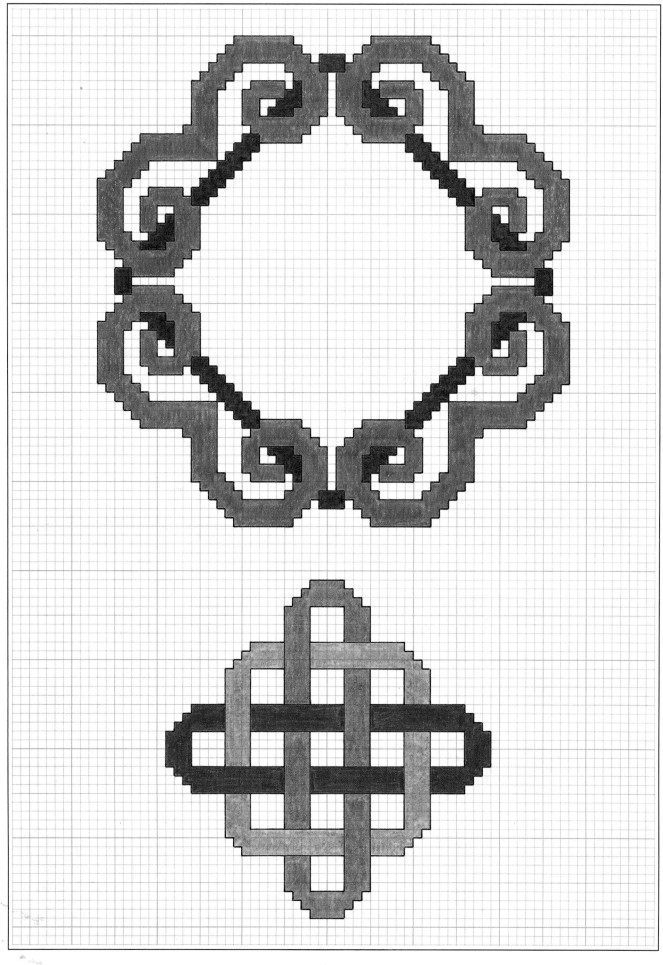

CHART 17

CHART 18

CHART 19

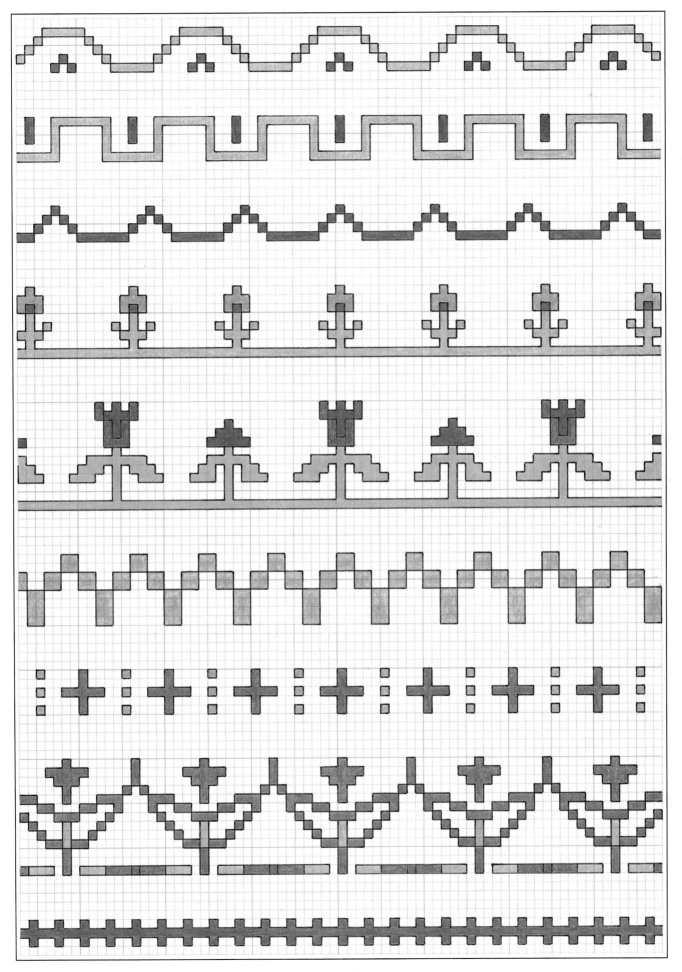

CHART 20

CHART 21

CHART 22

CHART 23

CHART 24

CHART 25

CHART 26

CHART 27

CHART 28

CHART 29

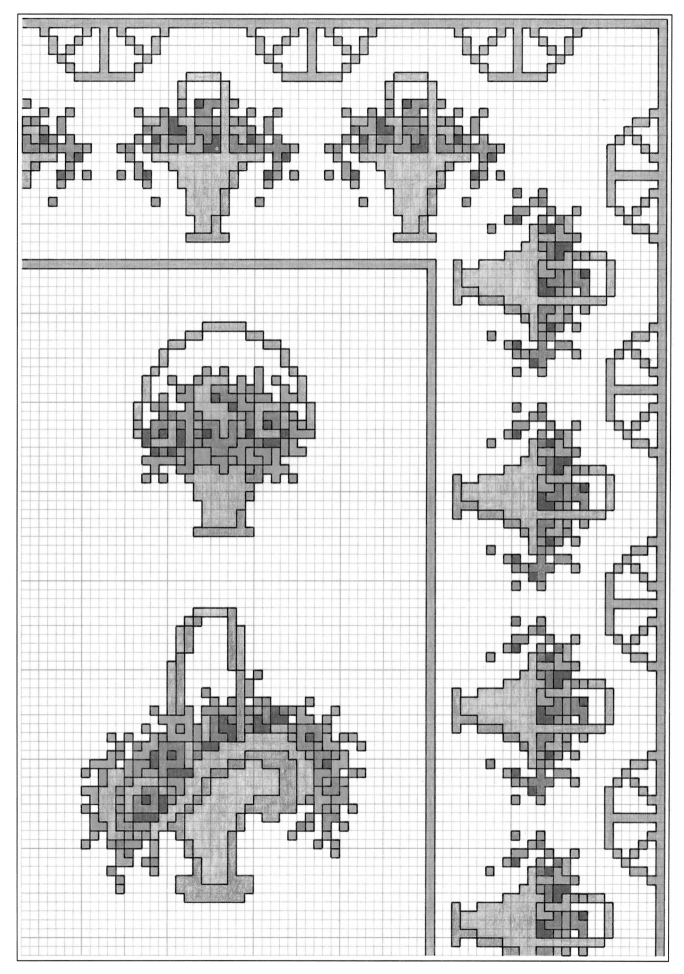

CHART 30

CHART 31

CHART 32

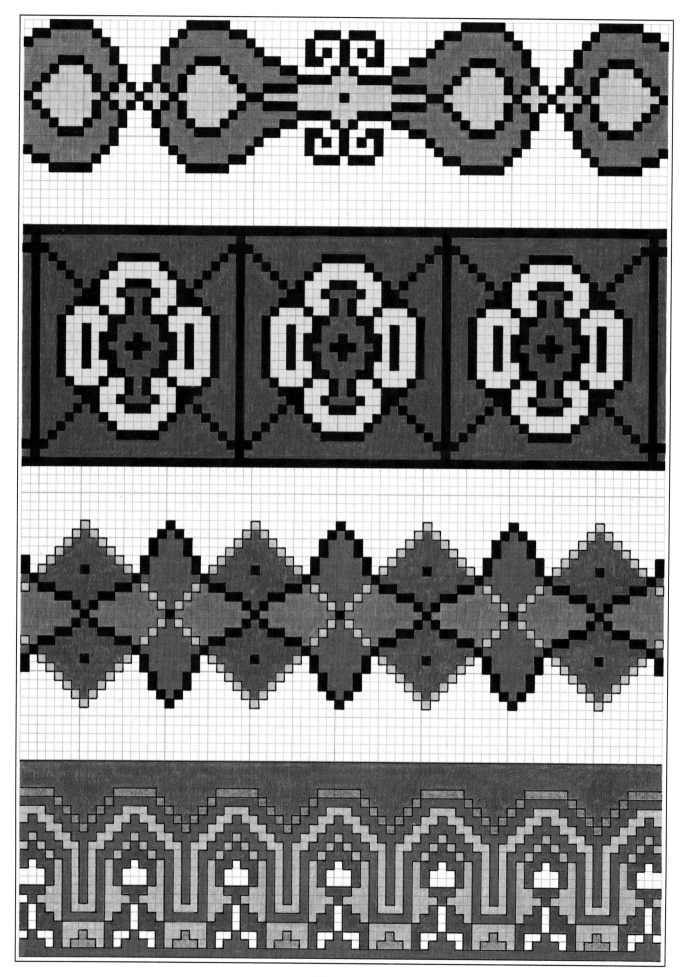

CHART 33

CHART 34

CHART 35

CHART 36

CHART 37

CHART 38

CHART 39

CHART 40

CHART 41

CHART 42

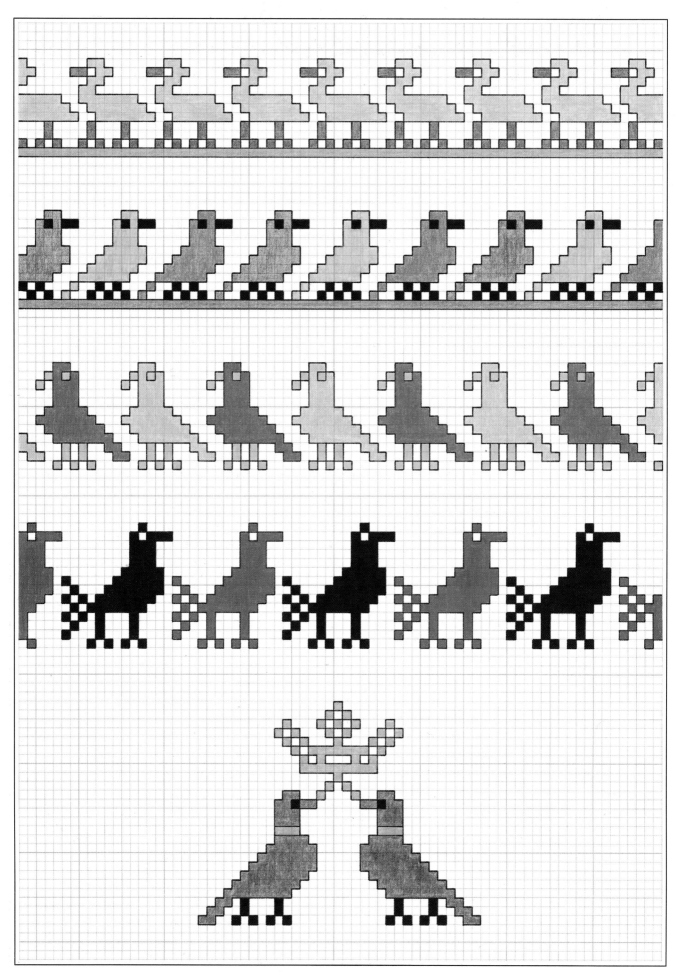

CHART 43

CHART 44

CHART 45

CHART 46

CHART 47

CHART 48

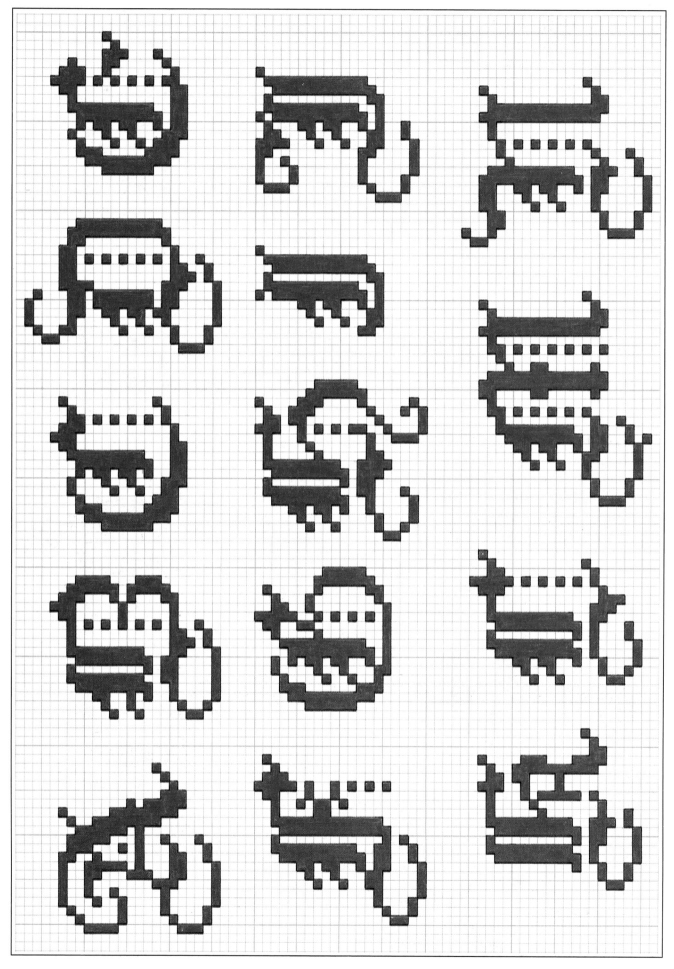

CHART 49

CHART 50

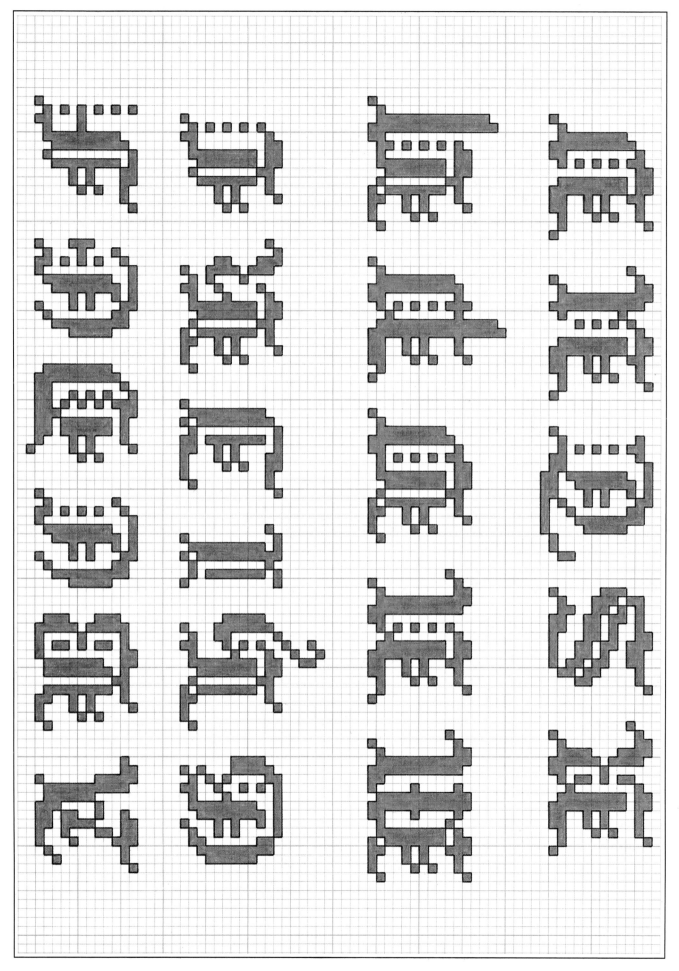

CHART 51

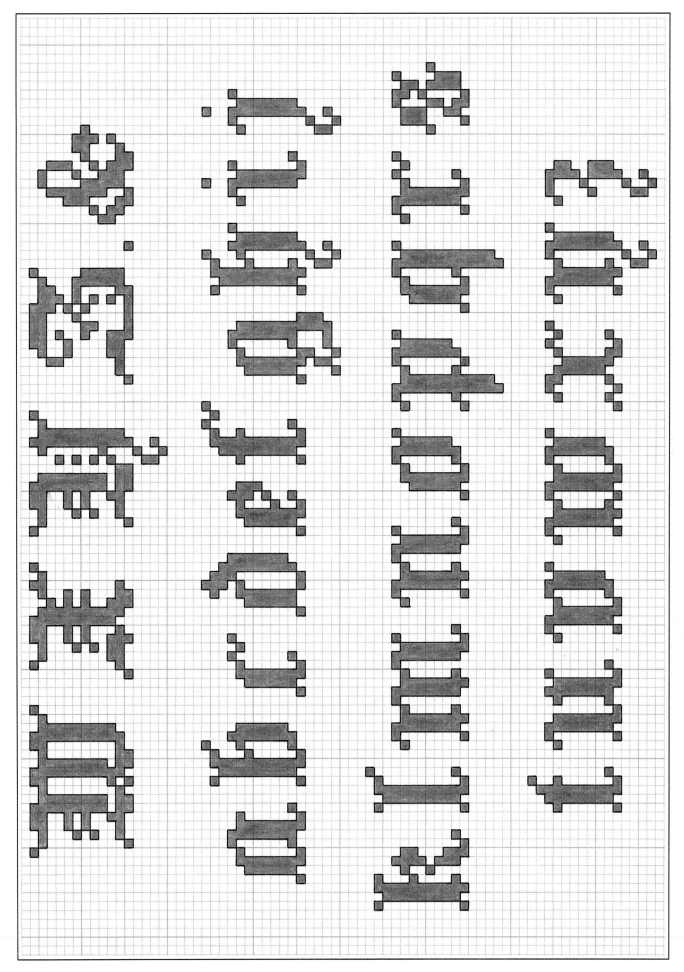

CHART 52

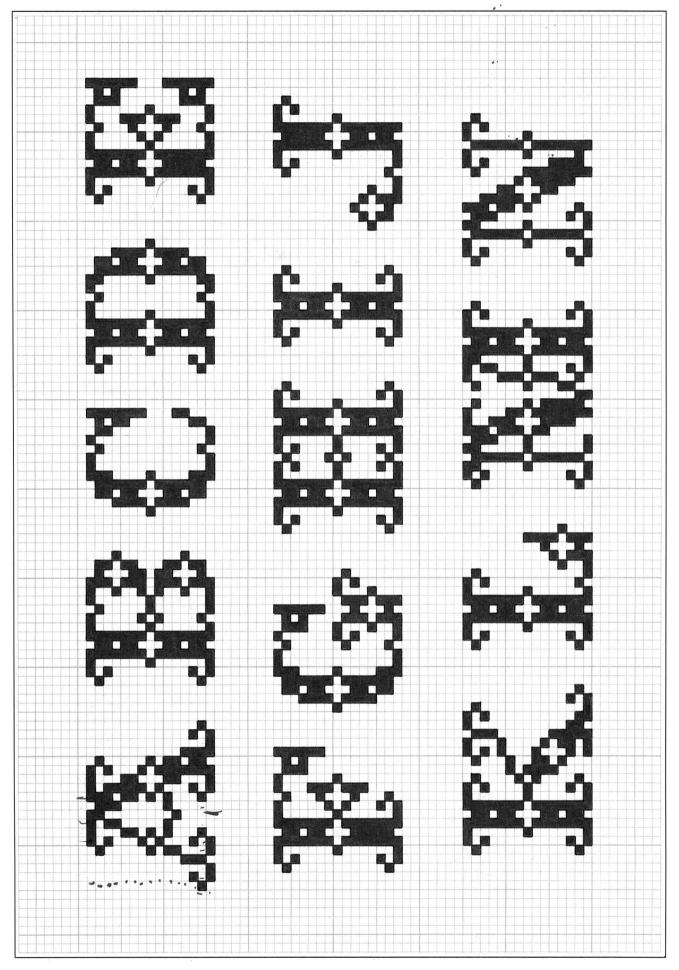

CHART 53

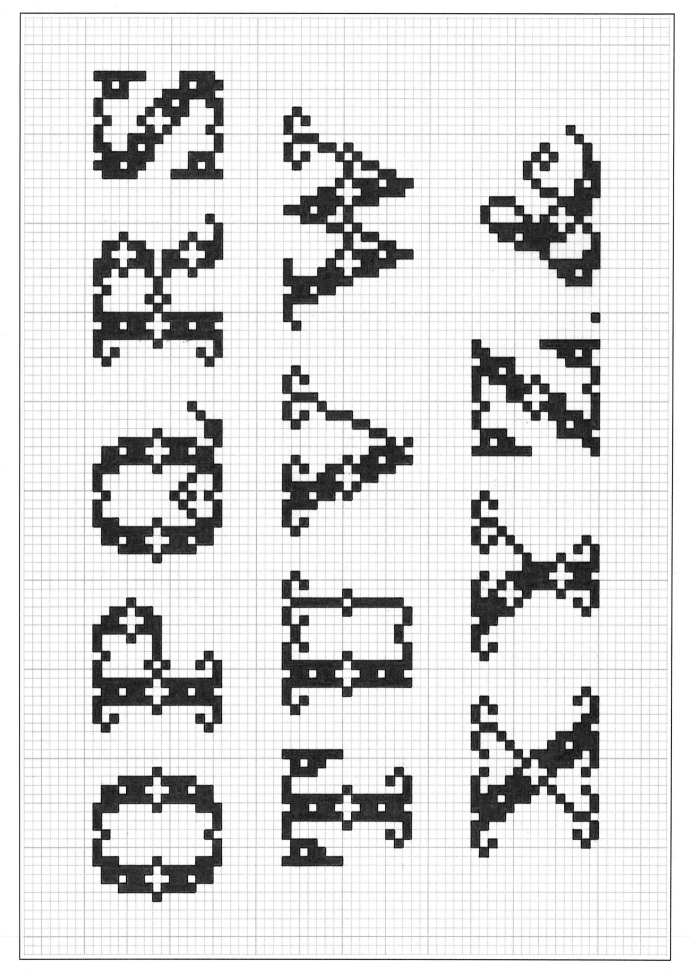

CHART 54

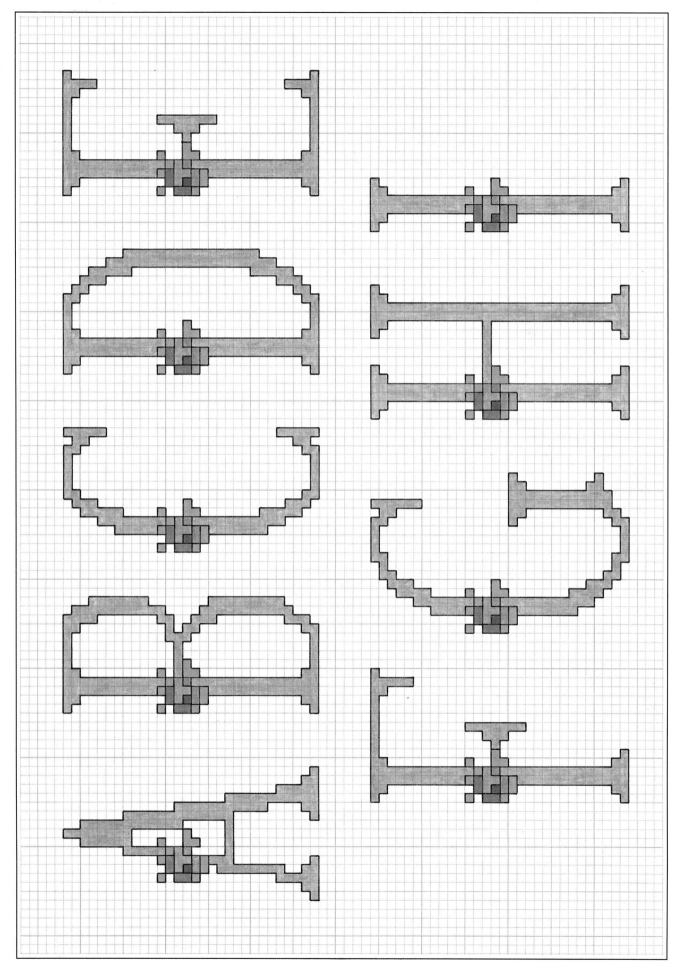

CHART 55

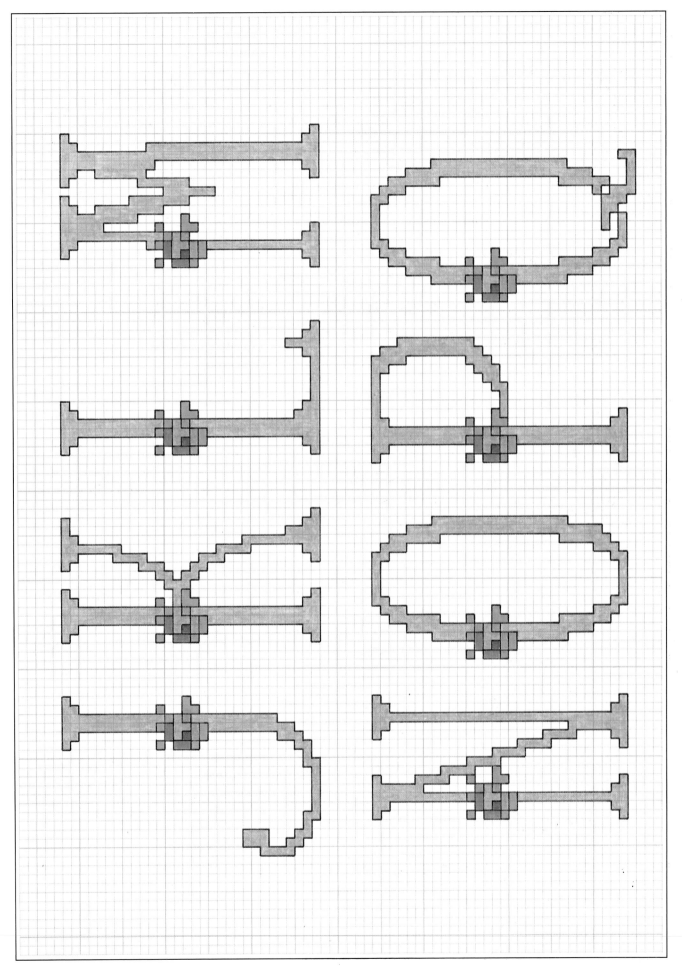

CHART 56

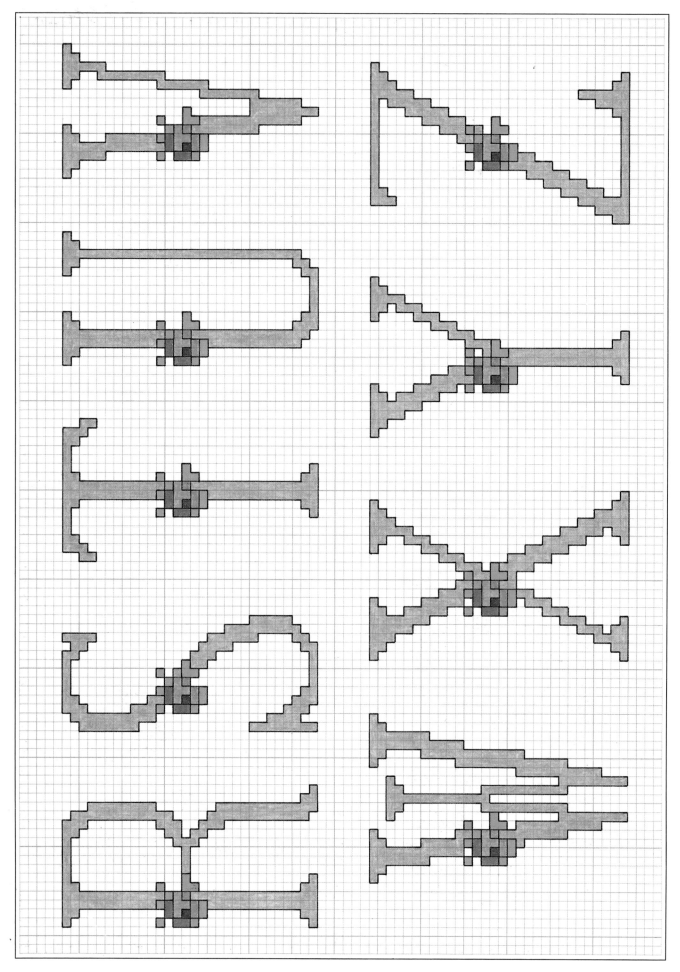

CHART 57

CHART 58

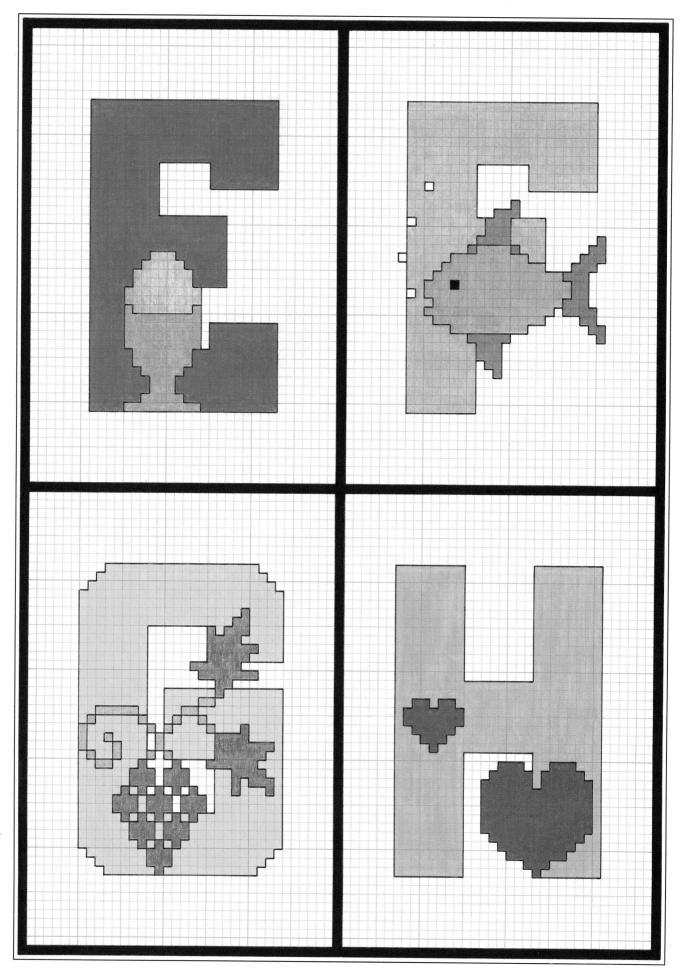

CHART 59

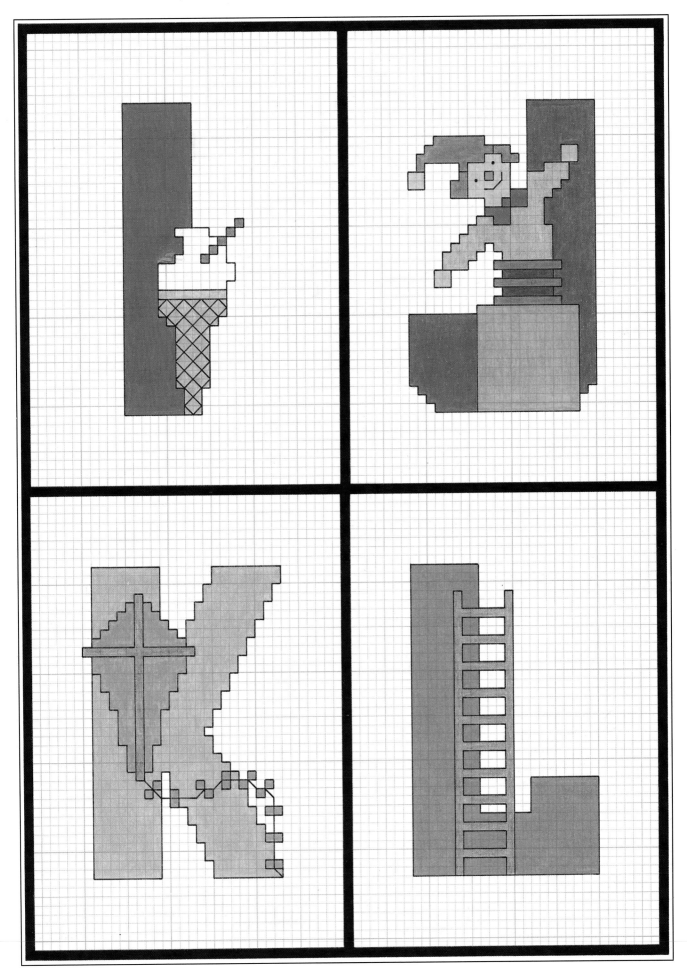

CHART 60

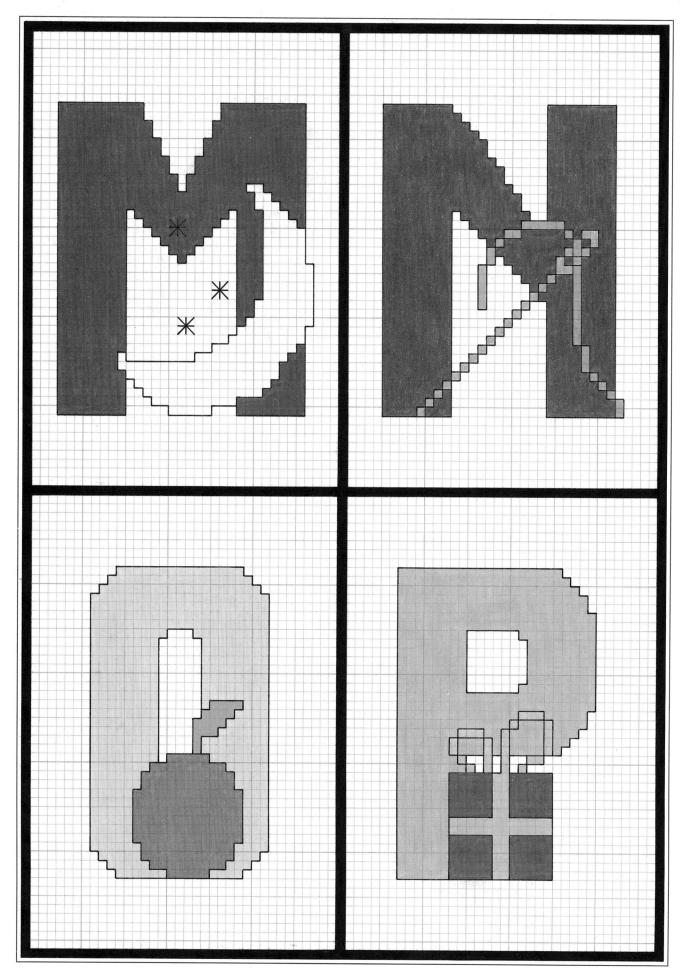

CHART 61

CHART 62

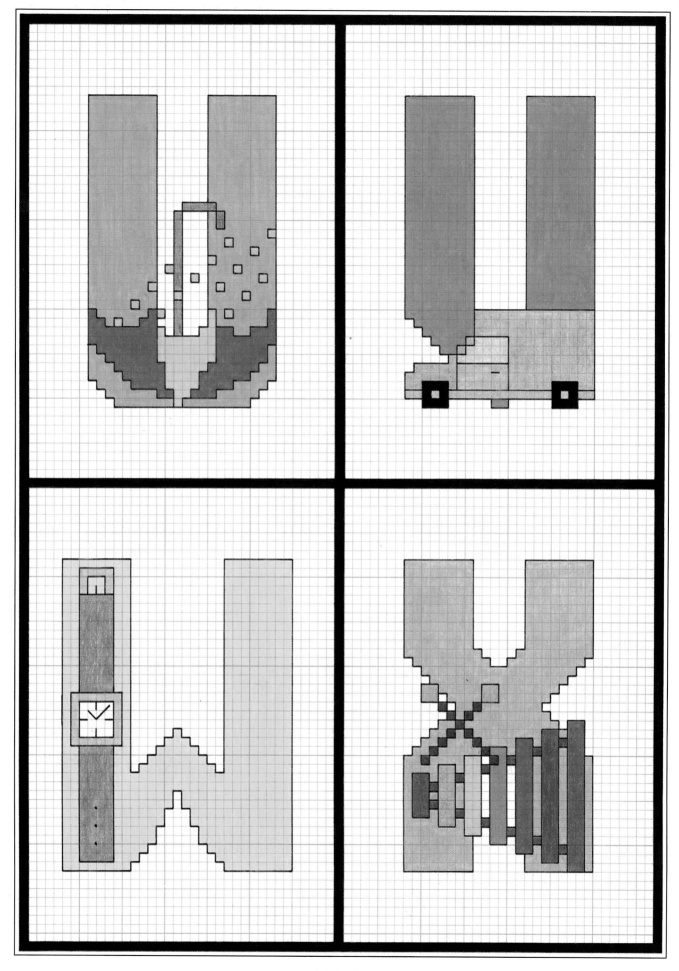

CHART 63

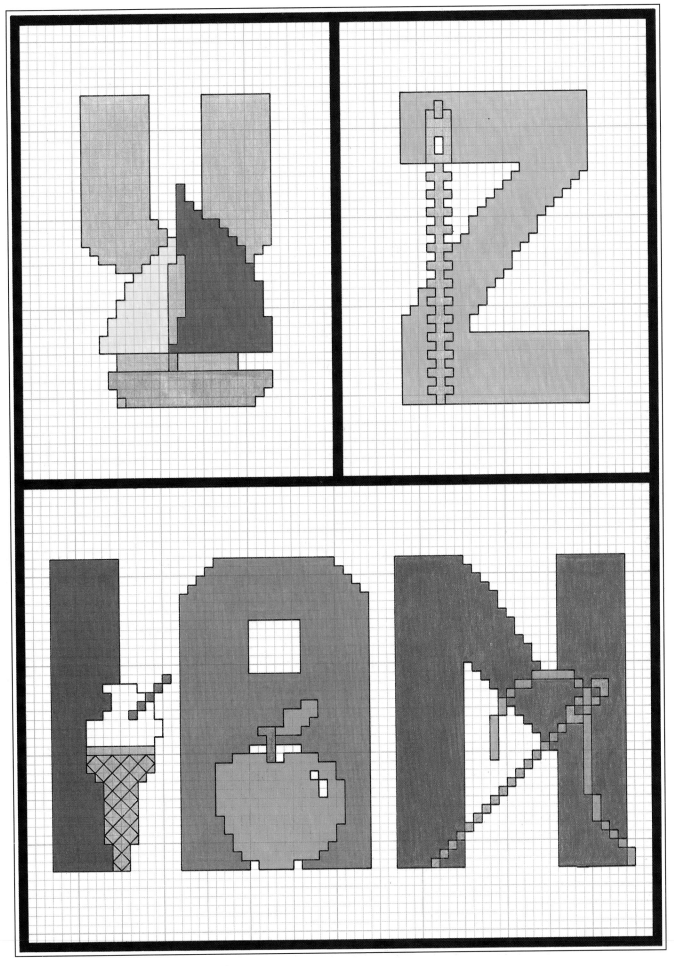

CHART 64

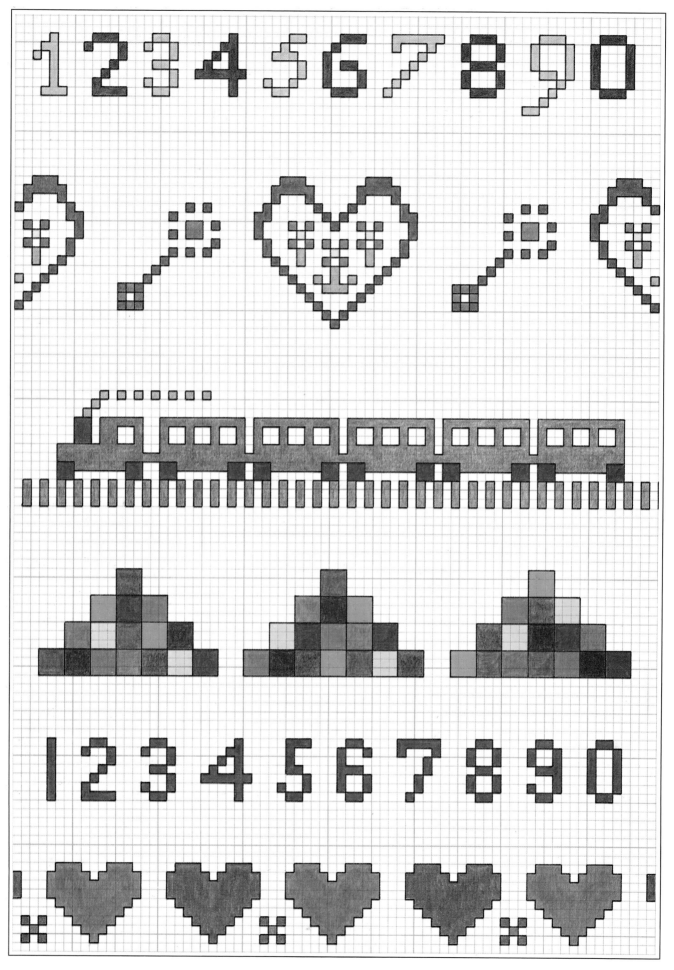

CHART 65

CHART 66

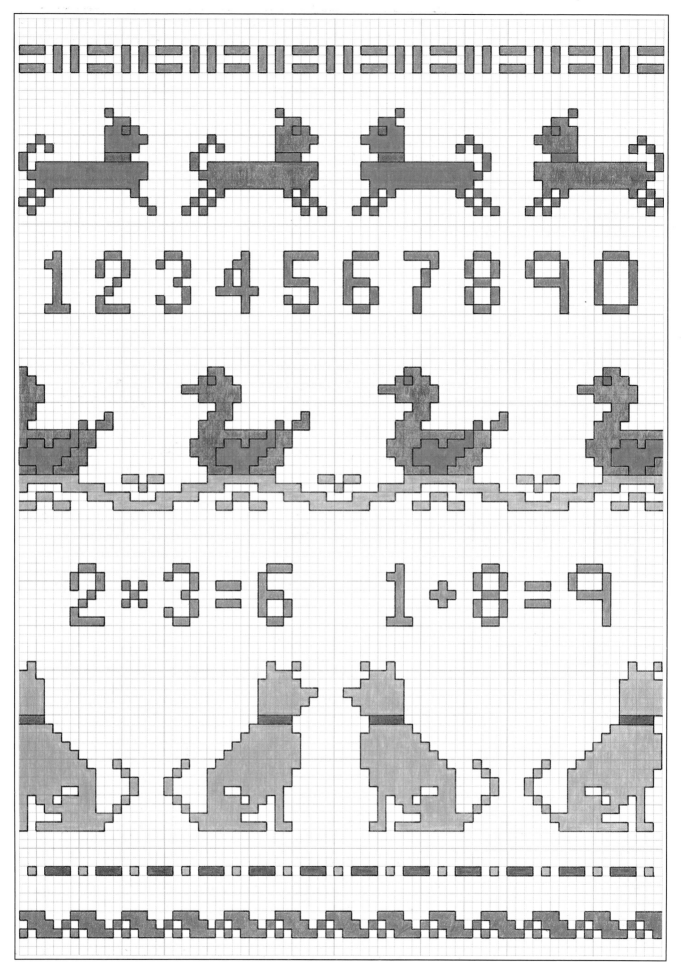

CHART 67

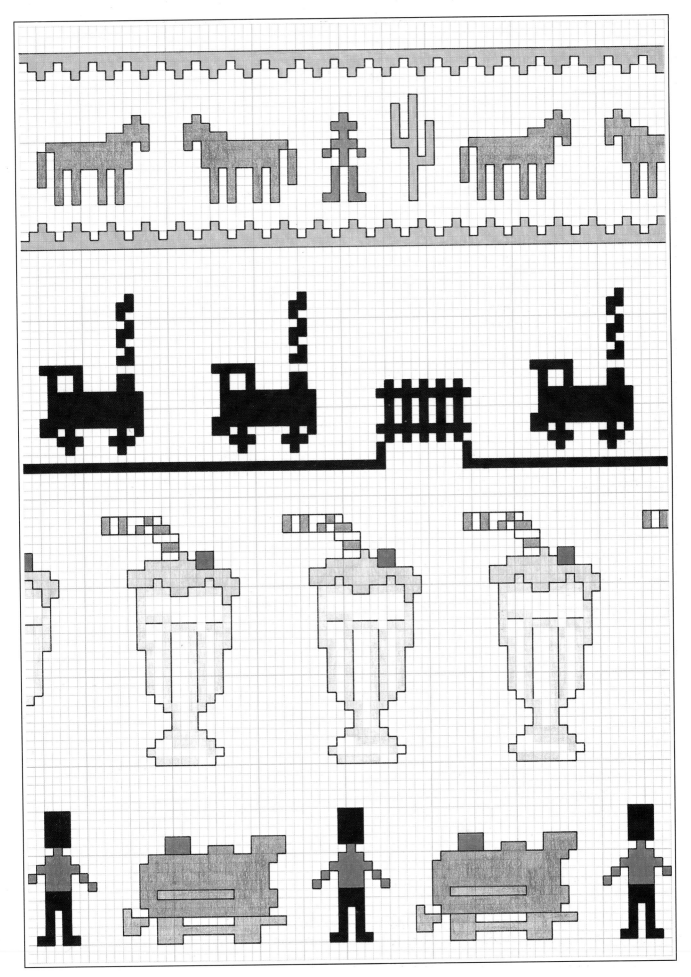

CHART 68

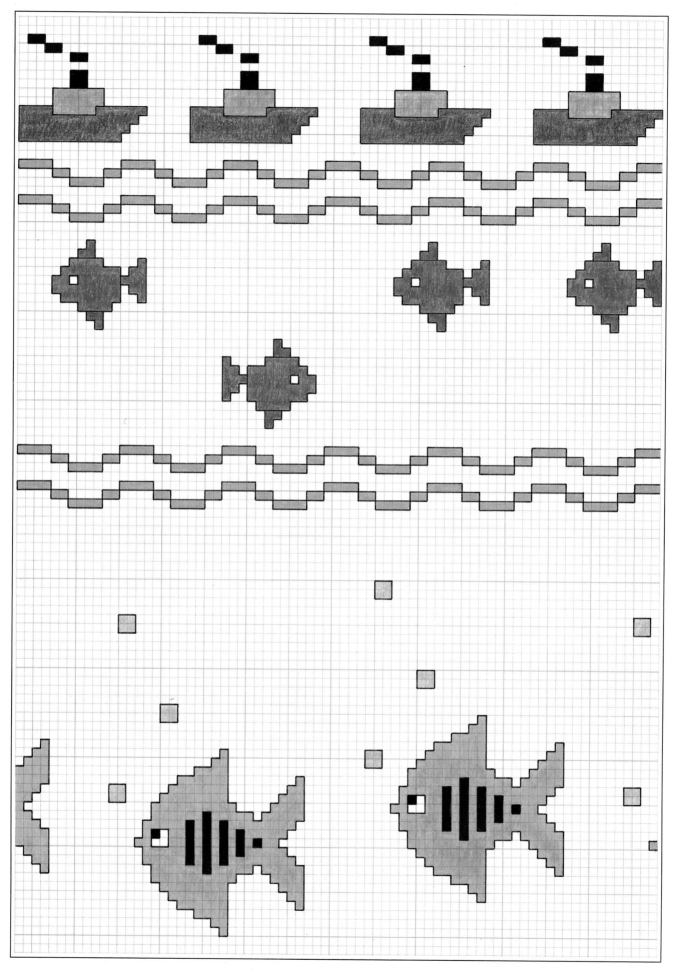

CHART 69

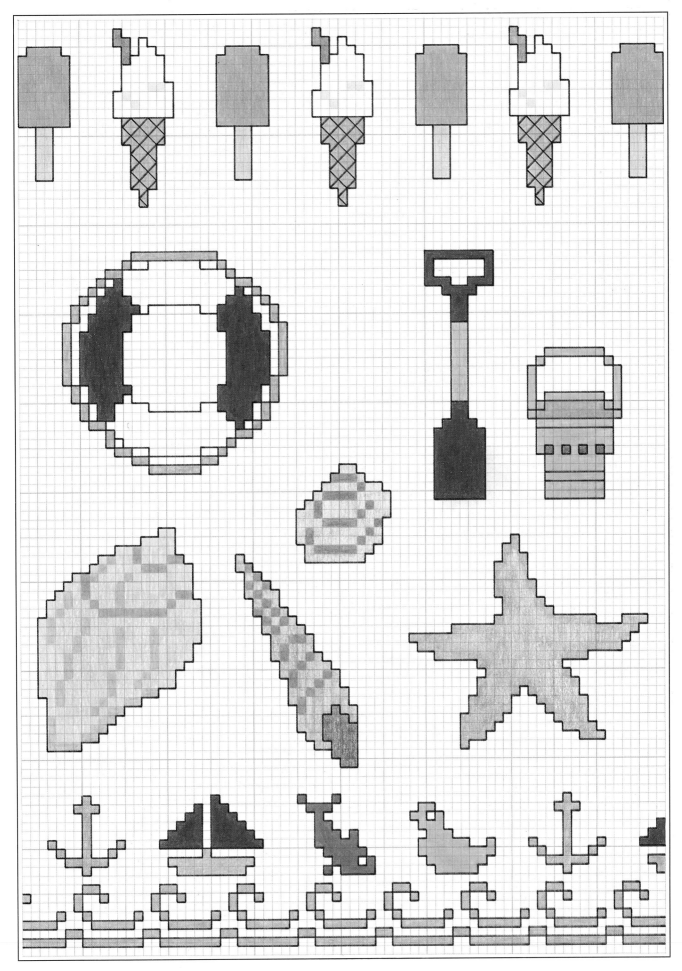

CHART 70

CHART 71

CHART 72

CHART 73

CHART 74

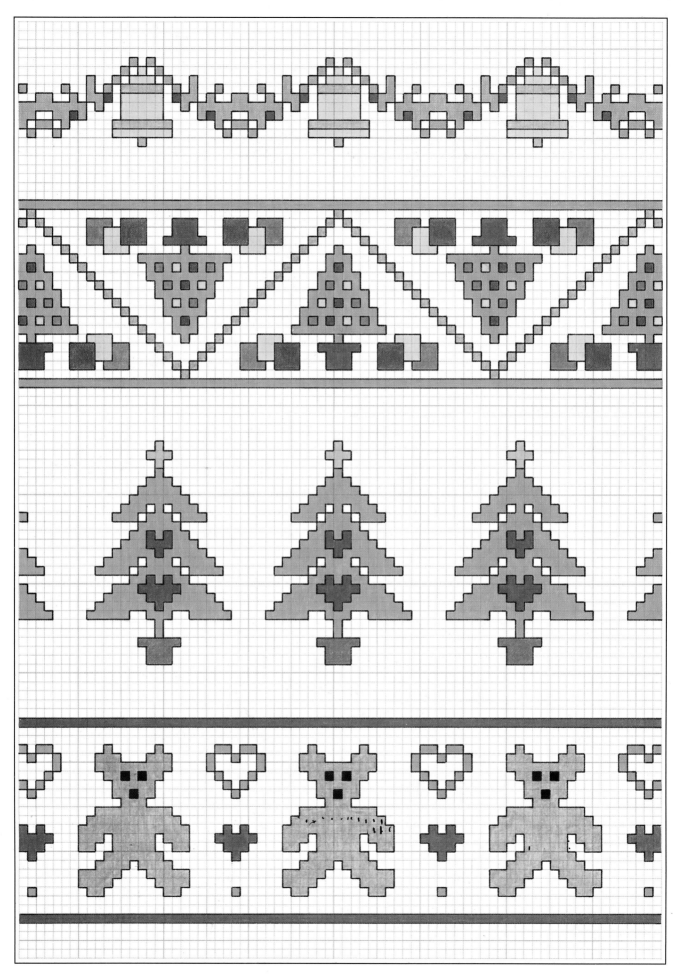

CHART 75

CHART 76

CHART 77

CHART 78

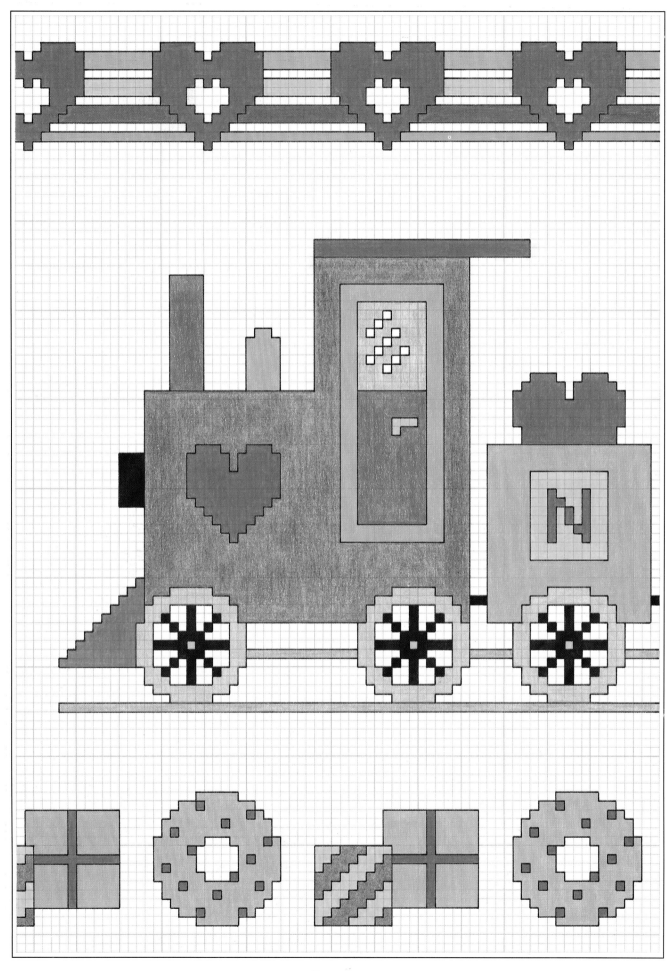

CHART 79

CHART 80

CHART 81

CHART 82

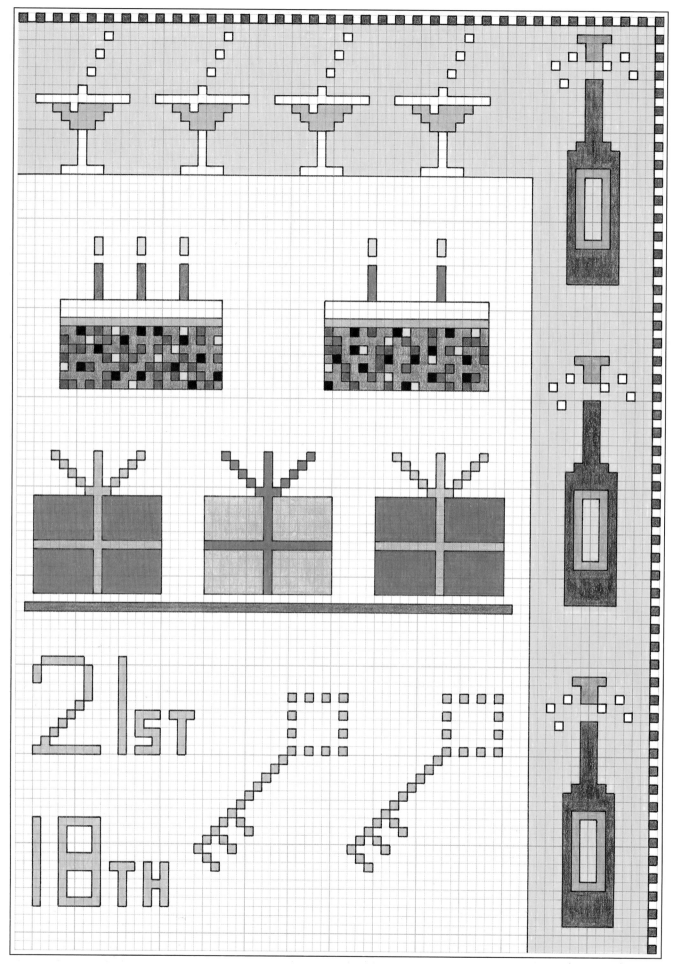

CHART 83

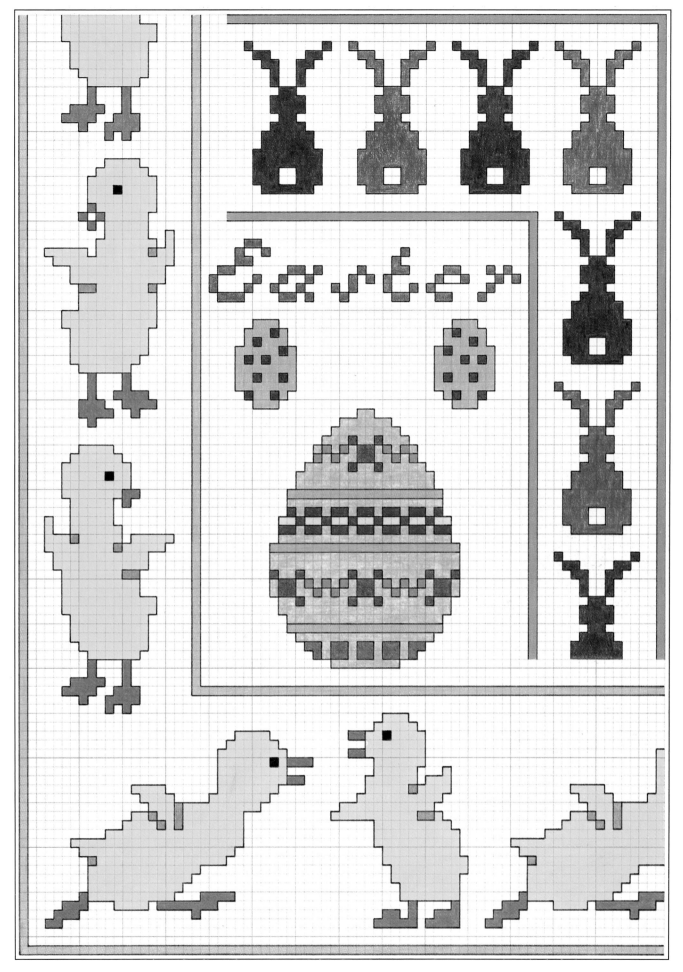

CHART 84

CHART 85

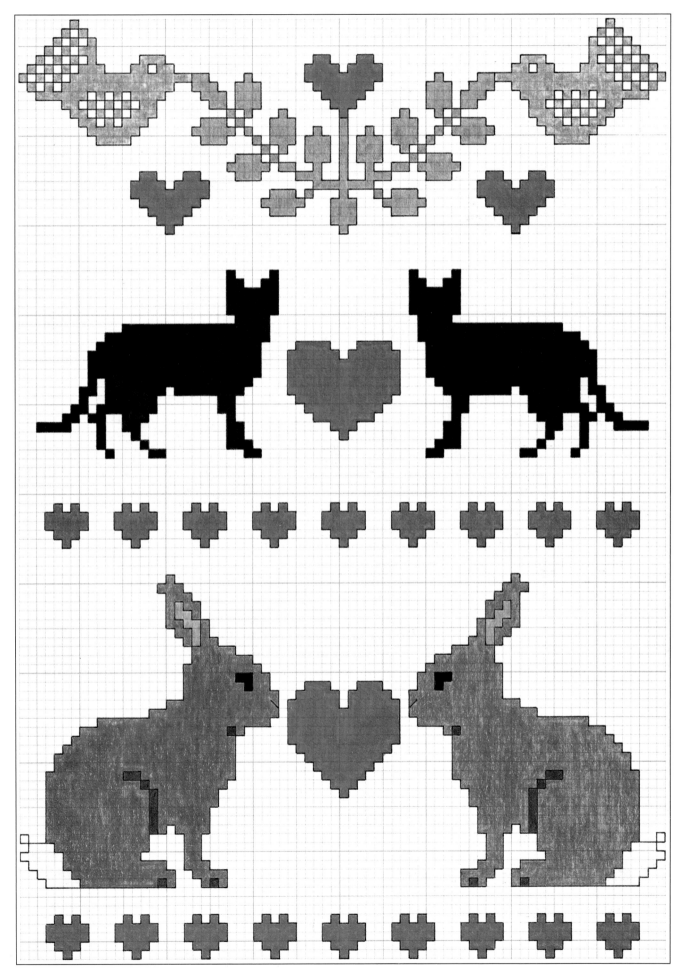

CHART 86

CHART 87

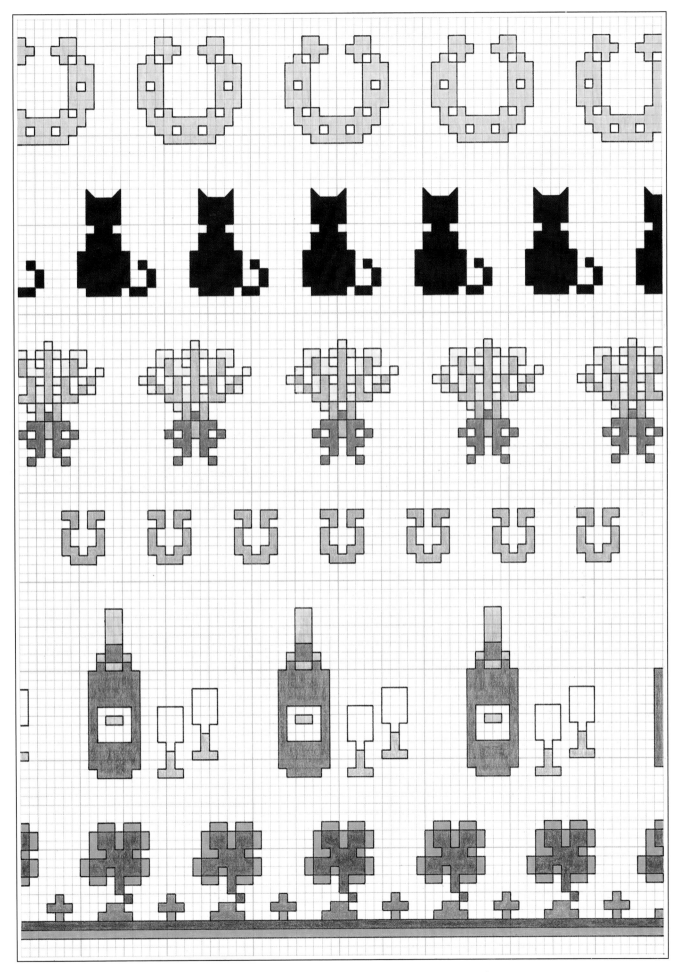

CHART 88

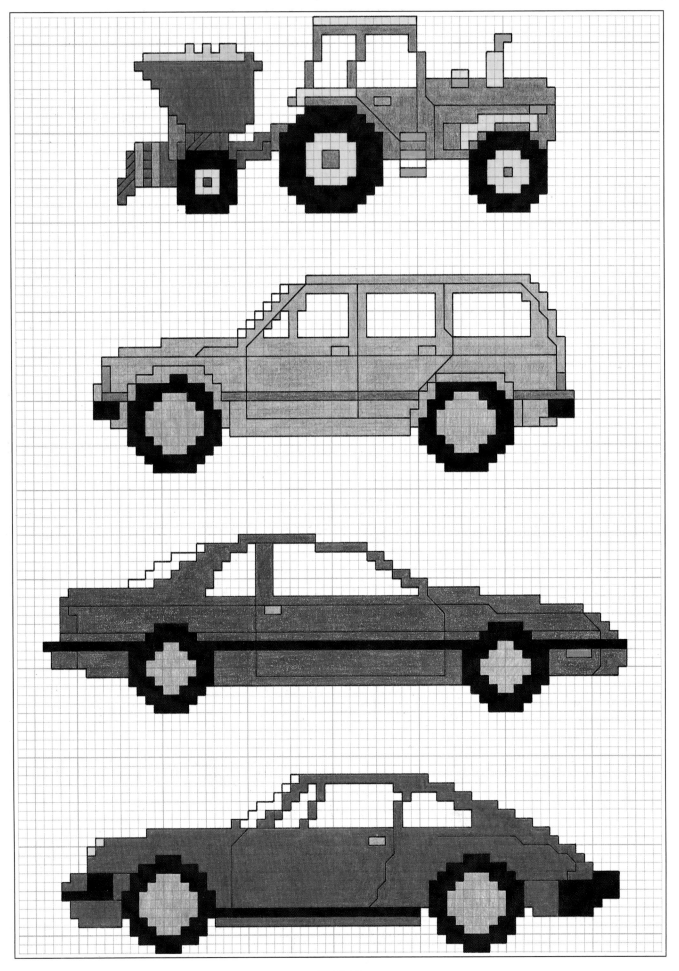

CHART 89

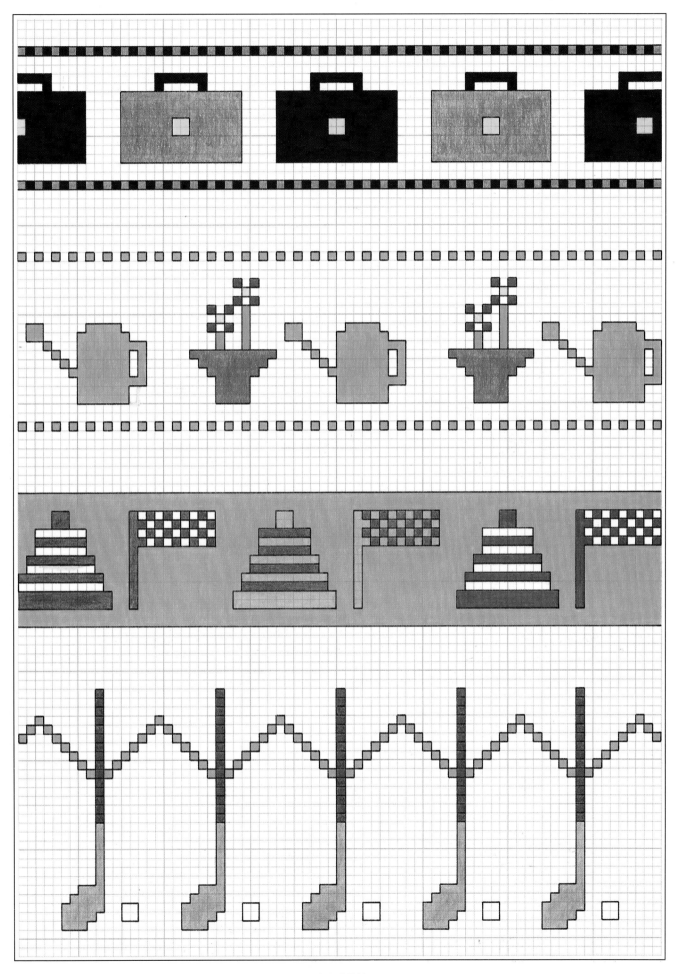

CHART 90

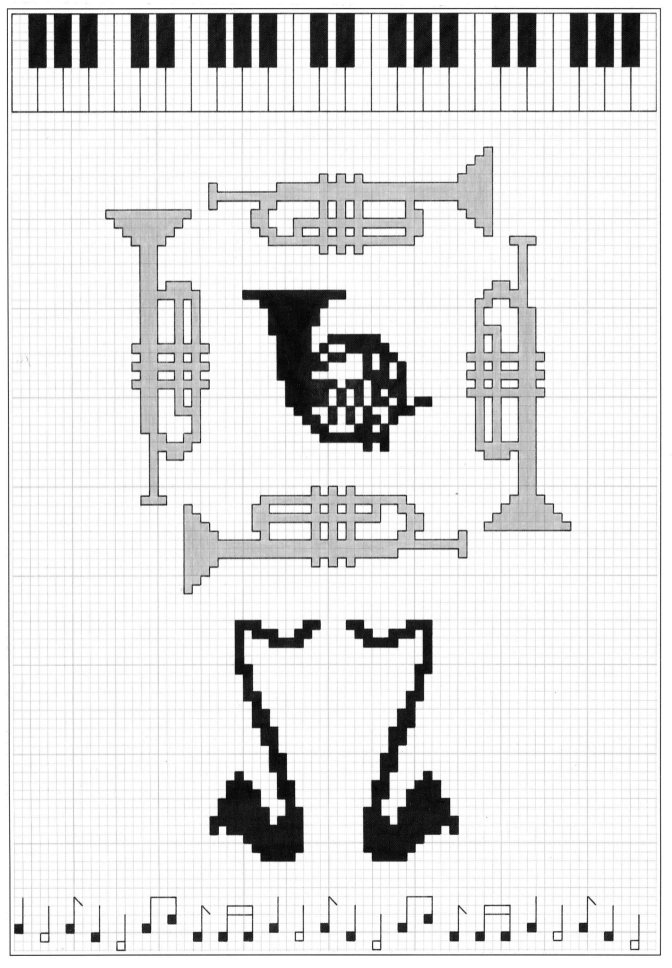

CHART 91

CHART 92

CHART 93

CHART 94

CHART 95

CHART 96

CHART 97

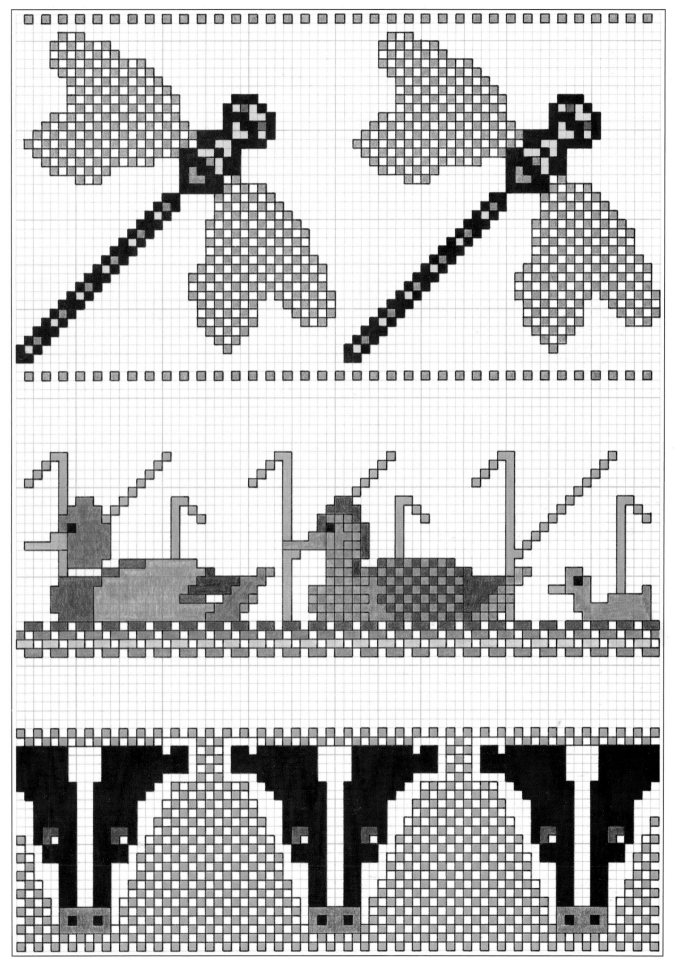

CHART 98

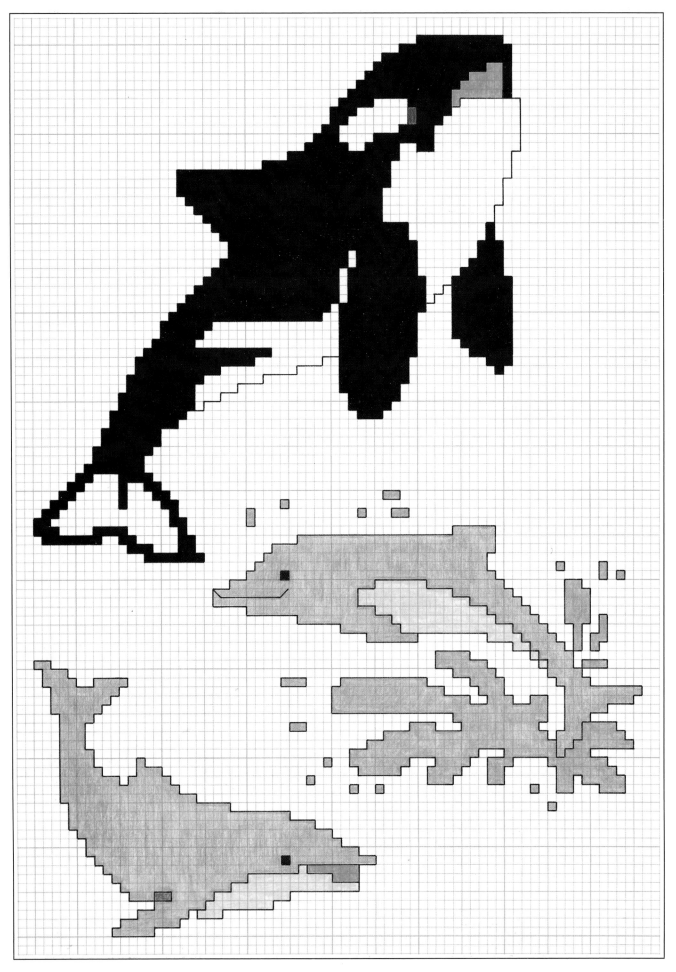

CHART 99

CHART 100

CHART 101

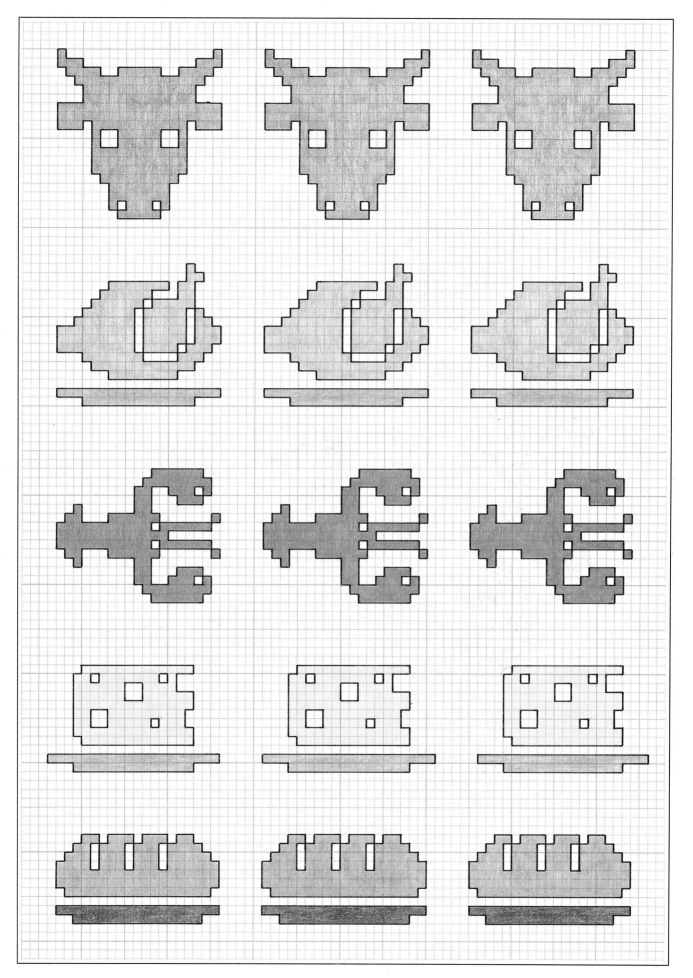

CHART 102

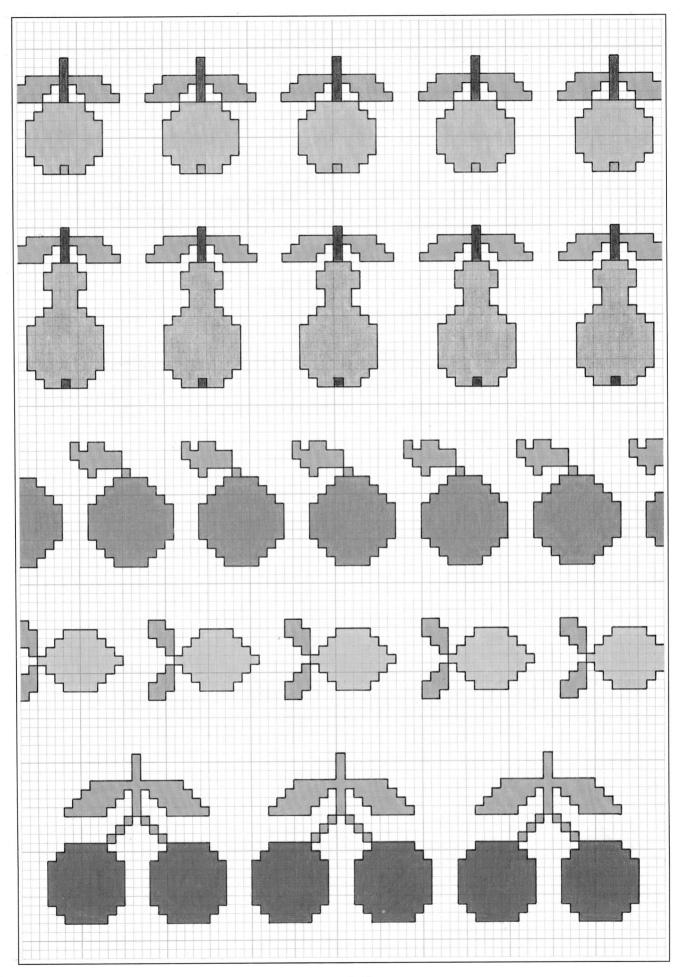

CHART 103

CHART 104

CHART 105

CHART 106

CHART 107

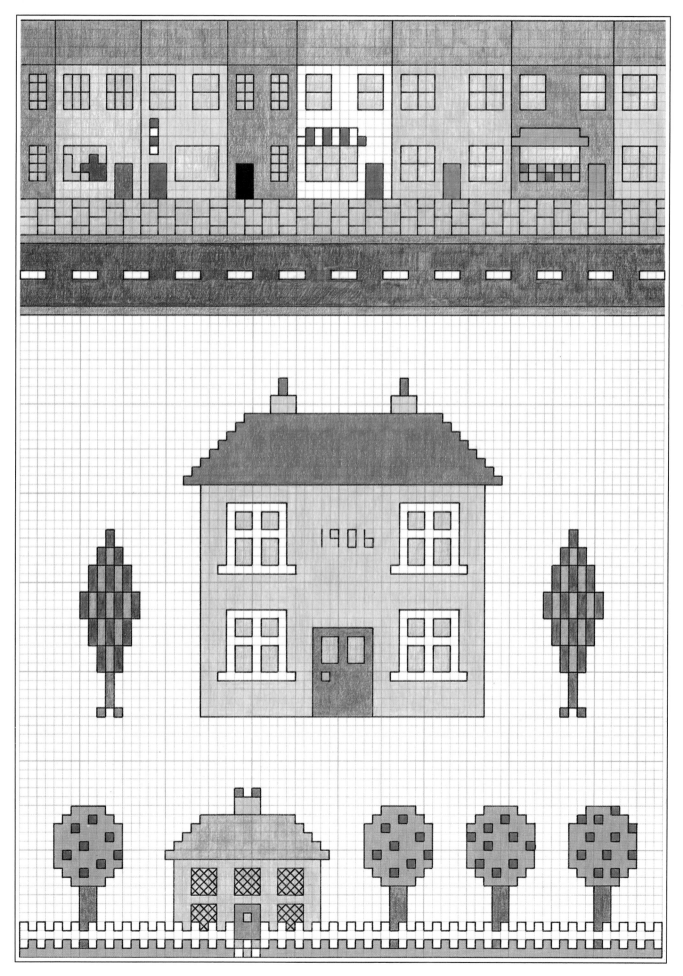

CHART 108

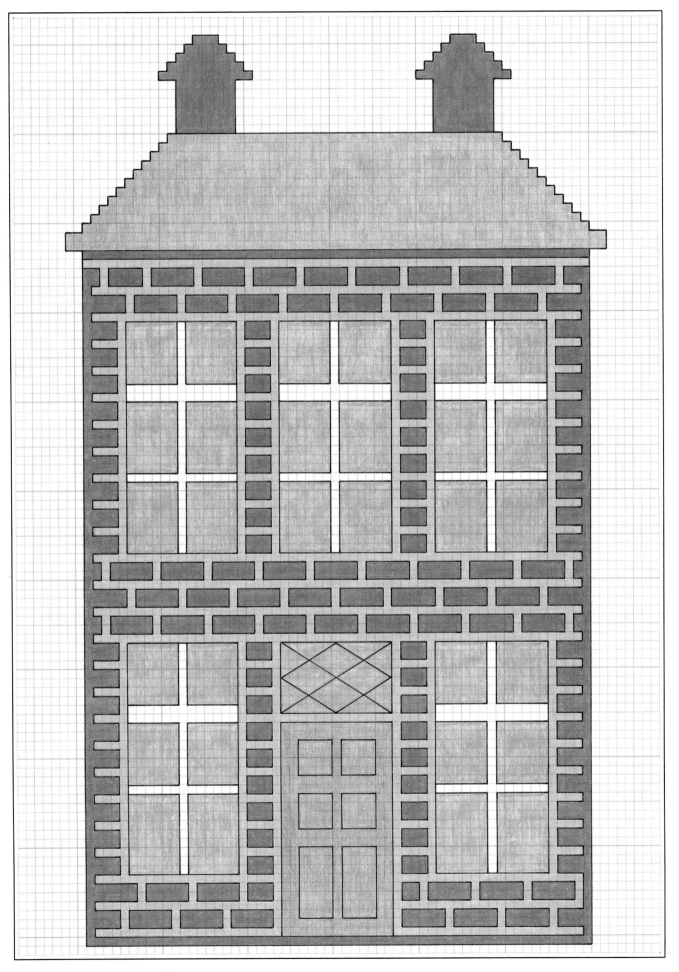

CHART 109

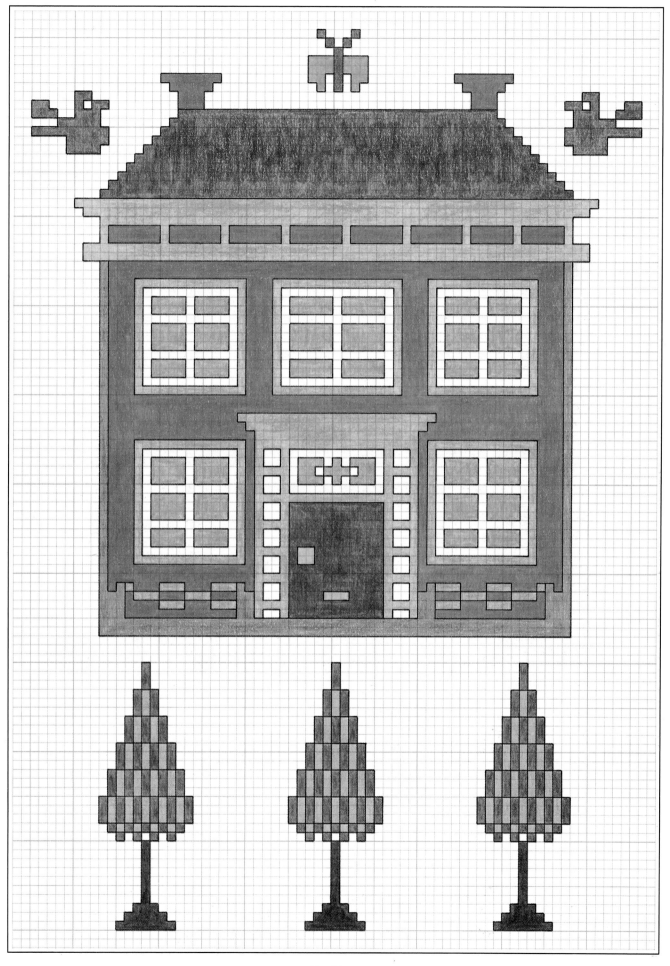

CHART 110

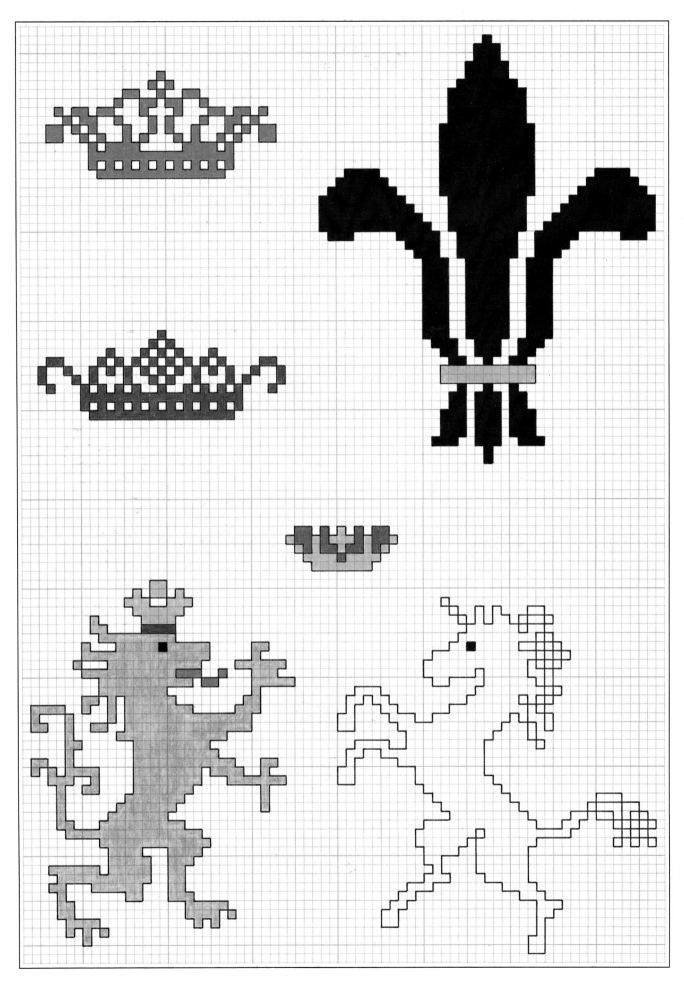

CHART 111

CHART 112

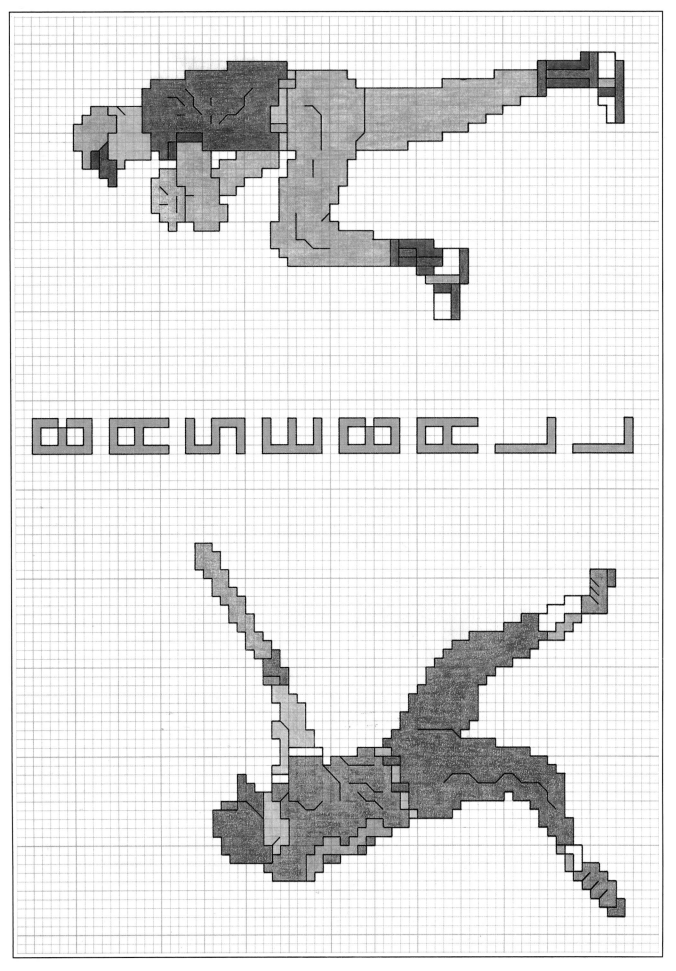

CHART 113

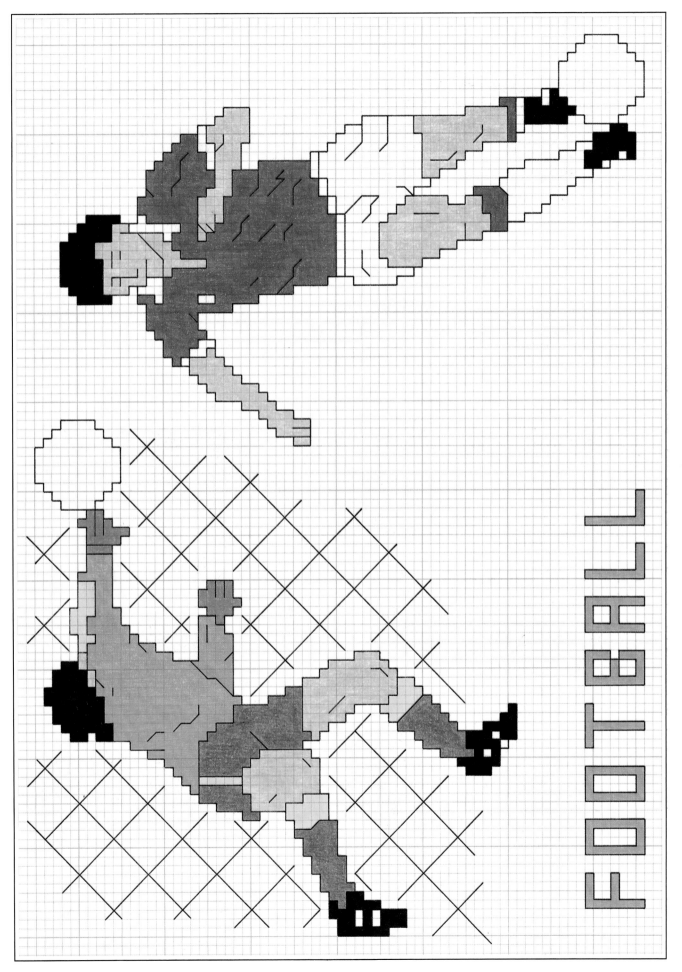

CHART 114

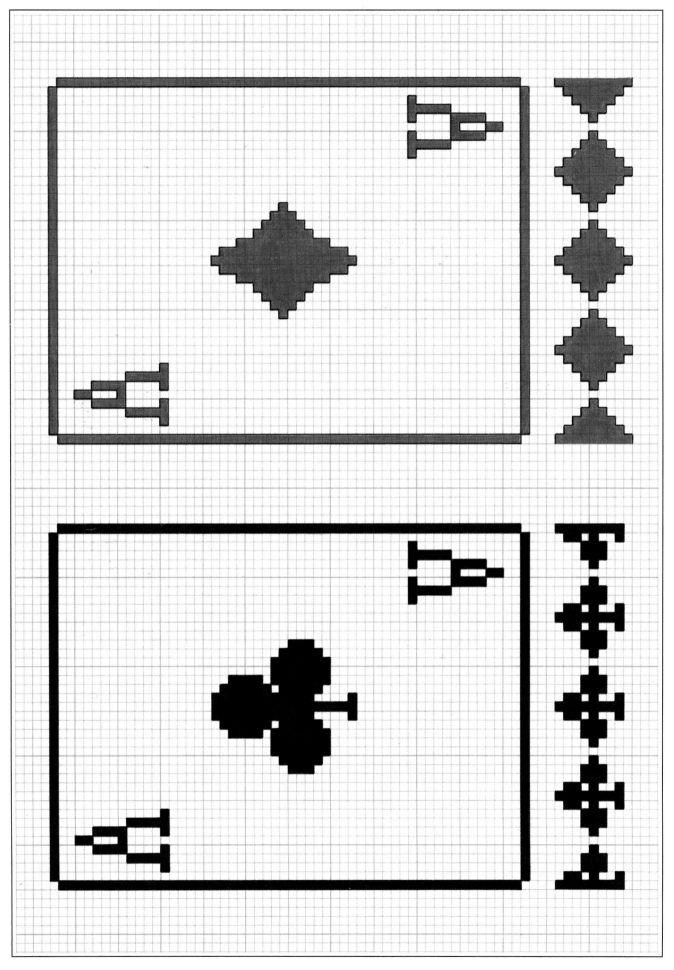

CHART 115

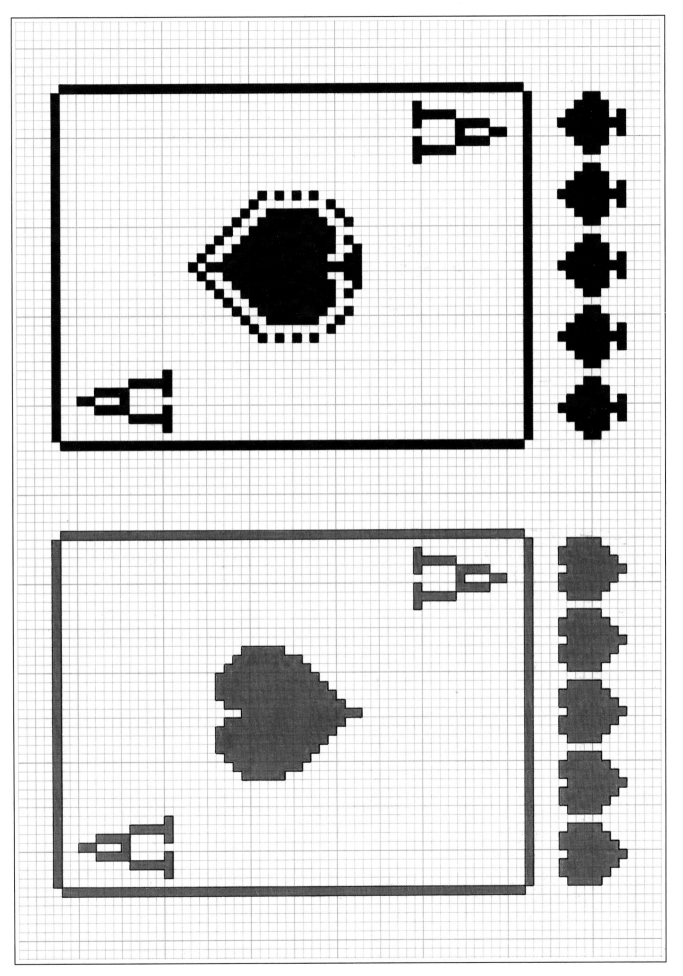

CHART 116

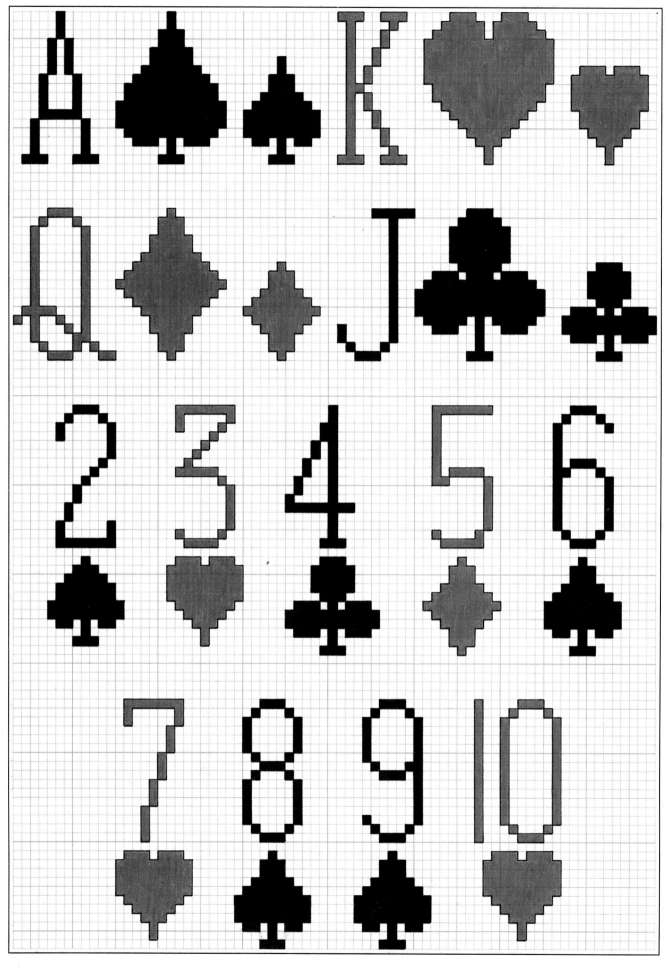

CHART 117

CHART 118

INDEX